THE PANIC FREE
JOB SEARCH

UNLEASH THE POWER OF THE WEB AND
SOCIAL NETWORKING TO GET HIRED

BY

PAUL HILL

CAREER
PRESS

THE CAREER PRESS, INC.
Pompton Plains, NJ

P9-CDW-957

Copyright©2012 by Paul Hill

All rights reserved under the Pan-American and International Copyright Conventions. This book may not be reproduced, in whole or in part, in any form or by any means electronic or mechanical, including photocopying, recording, or by any information storage and retrieval system now known or hereafter invented, without written permission from the publisher, The Career Press.

THE PANIC FREE JOB SEARCH
EDITED BY JODI BRANDON
TYPESET BY NICOLE DEFELICE
Cover design by Wes Youssi
Printed in the U.S.A.

To order this title, please call toll-free 1-800-CAREER-1 (NJ and Canada: 201-848-0310) to order using VISA or MasterCard, or for further information on books from Career Press.

CAREER
PRESS

The Career Press, Inc.
220 West Parkway, Unit 12
Pompton Plains, NJ 07444
www.careerpress.com

Library of Congress Cataloging-in-Publication Data
Hill, Paul, 1961

The panic free job search : unleash the power of the web and social networking to get hired / by Paul Hill.

p. cm.
Includes bibliographical references and index.
ISBN 978-1-60163-203-6 -- ISBN 978-1-60163-616-4 (ebook) 1. Job hunting--Computer network resources. 2. Internet. 3. Online social networks. I. Title.

HF5382.7.H55 2012
650.14--dc23

2011046641

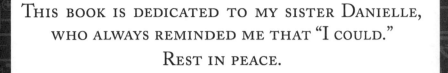

This book is dedicated to my sister Danielle, who always reminded me that "I could." Rest in peace.

ACKNOWLEDGMENTS

This book was made possible by the loving support and encouragement of the following people:

My family, for the incredible patience and understanding they demonstrate and their support throughout the project; Nicholas, Justin, Eric, and of course the angel Trish. My brother, Marc, and sisters, Lise, Martine, (Danielle), Jeanne, Leslie, and Andree.

Navgeet Bajaj for her selfless and endless hours of work, dedication, support, encouragement, editing, re-editing, and total commitment to the project.

My mom and dad for supporting and encouraging me throughout the years and for setting the bar a little higher.

My agent, Herb Schaffner, for his friendship and great representation, and his superb ideas and direction in the proposal stages.

All my friends, thank you for the great ideas and encouragement, especially Chris Demerah for his support and words of inspiration and for being a lifelong friend for 43 years and counting. Jackie Hill who kept things organized. Chrysantha Xavier, Jay Mistry, Keith Dawson, and Robert Bafaro for their continuous encouragement.

All my clients and staff from ADV Advanced Technical Services Inc. and TransitiontoHired, present and past, from around the world for your dedication, friendship, support, and help throughout the years.

Libby Gill for her timely advice on becoming a published author. Lainy Phillips for all her work on the first draft of the manuscript. For the team at Career Press for believing in me.

Alex Mandossian and Kieron Sweeney for stepping up and making a key telephone introduction.

CONTENTS

Conclusion:

INTRODUCTION

YOUR WORK IS TO DISCOVER YOUR WORK AND THEN WITH ALL YOUR HEART TO GIVE
YOURSELF TO IT.

—BUDDHA[1]

What if you could wake up every morning energized and eager to take on your work challenges? What if you loved your job, work, or career? What if you could get the edge over your competition and land the job you really want? What if you could be irresistible to employers and have employers chasing after you? What if you could have financial security and never, ever have to look for another job again? Do you think you would be healthier, wealthier, and happier? Get ready to find out!

ARE YOU AFRAID OF LOSING THE JOB YOU HATE?

Recent surveys have shed light on just how discontented workers are with their jobs. As Lynn Franco states, in a revealing *Washington Post* article, "Tellingly, when asked to name the most enjoyable part of their jobs, the top answer—just above enjoying the company of co-workers—was the commute."[2] To add more despair to the situation, studies clearly show that job stress leads to major health risks. "A substantial body of evidence shows a strong correlation between workplace stress and the development of cardiovascular problems such as hypertension and myocardial infarction."[3]

This direct correlation between job stress and cardiovascular problems is just as deadly for women as it is for men, as new studies presented at the American Heart Association's Scientific Sessions 2010 clearly show. Not only do workers need to contend with the effects of job stress, but worrying about losing a job can raise heart risks, too, as researchers discovered in this same U.S. government–funded study.[4]

Did you order the "double job whammy" with a side of myocardial infarction?

If you are like most people, you are cutting your life short because you don't like your job. If that is not crazy enough, you are adding to your health risks because you are afraid to lose the job you hate. Come on! Are you serious? Is this any way to live? Think about it.

If you are not satisfied with your work, it is killing you.

I believe most people don't get the job they want because they do not know what they want! If they know what they want, they don't know how to get it! If they know what they want and they know how to get it, then they don't take the steps and action to get it.

This book will give you the gift of knowing what job you want, show you step-by-step how to get it, and energize you with the power to take the action to get it!

TRADITIONAL JOB SEARCH SUCKS!

When I ask professionals if they like doing a job search, the answer without hesitation is always a loud "*No. I hate it!*"

Would never, ever having to look for work again appeal to you? *Panic Free Job Search* is not about searching high and low for work but rather about creating your irresistible offer that employers are attracted to and are compelled to act on. It is about being a candidate without first being an applicant. By the end of this book you will have all the tools you need to create your irresistible offer through the development of your powerful Professional Internet Brand (ProfessionaliBrand) and the deployment of the Smart Search system. ProfessionaliBranding is about managing and promoting the message about who you are as a professional on the Internet. It is also about managing your online reputation; this is critical to getting hired today. Smart Search is about combining your ProfessionaliBrand with an innovative job search that gets you hired.

It would be foolish to assume that one job-search technique works for everyone. For most professionals, the combination of various strategies and technqiues work best. To some, networking, be it face to face or through social networking sites, is jsut not comfortable; the Internet and social sites are foreign lands they prefer not to visit. For others, building an online presence, complete with an active blog, a Website, a YouTube channel, a video resume, a Web TV show, and a flourishing social media presence is exactly what they want in order to attract employers. For these reasons this book offers various Smart Search strategies and you will find at least one that is right for you.

THE KEY TO NEVER, EVER HAVING TO LOOK FOR ANOTHER JOB AGAIN

Your powerful ProfessionaliBrand is the key to unlocking the "new job search," and when you do, employers will come looking for you.

How is this possible, you ask?

Job search on the Internet used to be about applying to advertisements on job boards and employer sites, and of course e-mailing resumes to hiring managers—the "click and send" approach. Although these still work to a much lesser extent, and mostly today for "commodity jobs,"[5] all are based on conveying your message through the confines of the traditional resume. The traditional resume does a poor job of telling the story of who you are. Employers will hire you only if they like you, and the only way to figure that out is if they get to know you and trust you. The Web offers the perfect conduit for giving employers all the information they need about you.

The Web and social networking provide the opportunity to promote the message about who you are as a professional in a multimedia-rich way that is engaging and captivating to employers. These advances in technology are powerful tools you can use to influence the professional opinion others have of you, including employers. The professional opinion others have of you is a causal factor for employers to act on and make you an offer when making hiring decisions, and social media is the perfect tool for providing this critical input.

The sum total of everything you say or do, what others say about you, and the opinion of you as a professional that can be found online is your ProfessionaliBrand. Your ProfessionaliBrand is capable of delivering a positive, engaging message 24/7 in ways that influence employers that a document/resume can simply not achieve. Job search is about search and the Web is about search. Being found on the Web is about search ranking and page ranking. Page ranking does not only depend on keywords. It also depends on your authority, substantiated by social signals about you as a professional (for example, testi-monials, endorsements, Likes and +1s, and followers). In the Web 2.0 world, social signals move the masses, and social signals also move employers. The positive weight of social signals about your ProfessionaliBrand is becoming an important factor to move employers to offer you a job. In other words, how well you are liked and respected professionally by others is a strong signal to employers to chase after you or pass on you.

Who the Heck Is Paul Hill, and What the Heck Does He Know About Job Search?

My name is Paul Hill. I have placed thousands of professionals in the best jobs of their careers, and won numerous National Personnel Associates awards for my record of accomplishment. As an entrepreneur I have trained and taught thousands of unemployed and employed professionals and exec-utives the inside secrets and motivational system outlined in this book, the GetHiredFastTrack System. I know this: What I teach and coach works. Over and over again, clients and associates deploy my system, take smart action, and get hired. They forget the job boards and the online postings, and reach the decision-makers. They get the interviews and job offers they thought would never come their way.

Many books will teach you about passion, or self-confidence, or job search—but no book shows you all three with a specific emphasis on how to use innovative tools and processes that get you hired. This book will guide you through a system called A-C-T: *alignment, confidence,* and *tactics.* The book gives you a system for overcoming your fears and anxieties to become focused on an achievable goal. It provides research and marketing secrets that will help you reach the hidden job market, and it shows you how to attract employers with your irresistible offer, through ProfessionaliBranding, so you will never, ever have to look for a job again.

Part I introduces you to revolutionary technology to put you on the path to success in the personal and professional aspects of your life. Part I also demonstrates the importance of choosing work by looking inward and making sure it is *aligned* with your interests and the things that drive you, such as passion, as well as the consequences of not doing so.

Part II builds *confidence* by guiding you to discover what you really want to do, your dreams, and how to set smart goals to reach your dreams. You are introduced to powerful mindful visualization techniques in order to overcome fear, shame, and reluctance to step up and go for your dream and the job that is right for you.

Part III contains *tactics* and mechanics to get you hired, including Google search strings, LinkedIn best practices, techniques for getting noticed by decision-makers and hiring managers, presentation marketing, Job Search Talking, building your irresistible offer through your ProfessionaliBrand, social networking, and other unique Smart Search best practices, from killer resumes to compensation negotiation.

If you are seeking your first serious job, are unemployed, or have a need for a more fulfilling opportunity or a career change, this book will help you. Smart Search will provide you with tangible results, and you will get hired by implementing my suggestions and methodology.

I wrote this book because my passion is my mission, and my mission is:

➡ To inspire people to get clarity on what they want, then show them how to get it.

➡ To inspire people to uncover their interests and what drives them— in essence, their passion—as well as their professional uniqueness, and by doing so enable them to take control of their work lives.

➡ To give professionals the freedom of never, ever having to look for another job again, and the rewards of getting a job they actually want, instead of a job that is simply available to them.

No longer do you have to settle for the job that is available to you simply because you need a paycheck. Nor is it about what is hot or good, but rather about what excites you and what you can make money at, while getting a thrill.

This book will provide you with the system and tools you can use to figure out what you want and how to get it. Throughout this book you will be invited to take—maybe even coerced into taking—action. In these pages, and additionally at TransitionToHired.com, I provide a field-tested system professionals have discovered that delivers results, as well as many more important inspirational truths (such as "getting off your duff" and doing something about finding a job!). If you follow through and take action, you will retain much of the information and set in motion a system that will guarantee your income and turn you into a proactive job-seeker always ready to entertain the multiple employment offers coming your way. Impossible, you say? Read on and get ready for an eye-opening and life-changing adventure. I ask for one commitment and that is to pledge to read the book from cover to cover, and then to help out other professionals by educating them and passing on the gift of this book so that we can help put this great country back to work. One last thing: Of course this is a serious subject, but hell—if you can't take a joke find another book!

PART I

ALIGNMENT

CHAPTER 1

TAMING THE INNER BEAST

To enjoy good health, to bring true happiness to one's family, to bring peace to all, one must first discipline and control one's own mind. If a man can control his mind he can find the way to Enlightenment, and all wisdom and virtue will naturally come to him.

—Buddha[1]

Looking for a job is a tough thing: true or false? True if you believe it is, and false if you have the right tools to give you certainty and confidence. Leaving a good job to pursue your dream, or losing a stable, long-term job can present some psychological challenges. Feelings of rejection, failure, and fear creep into everyone's psyche at times and can stop you from moving forward, and will remain there unless you know how to turn those feelings around.

Armed with the right tools, you can get the job you want regardless of whether you are employed and want something better or you are unemployed and desperate. First, you need to overcome the things that are holding you back. Perhaps it is a loss of confidence or negativity that is holding you back and instead you need to embrace new horizons. Tools that unravel the mysteries of the human brain have come a long way throughout the years, to the point where today's technology can be used to enhance one's performance. You can use very affordable technology breakthroughs to gain an advantage over your competition, and to get your brain truly reprogrammed and motivated to take on the stress and challenges of job search. It is not *Star Trek*; the technology exists and is readily available to you, as you will soon find out.

A Familiar Story: Kicked to the Curb

In my work as a job-search consultant, I have observed that a loss of a job is often accompanied by a temporary or persistent loss in confidence that affects the individual's ability to land a job. To illustrate this fact, here is a typical story I have heard many times repeated to me through my work as a job-search consultant.

You have worked at a company for more than 10 years. The new young guy you hate is retained by your organization, and you are shown the exit. As you insist on heading back to your desk to get your stuff, the management team tells you they will pack up your personal belongings and send them to you at home. You are now outraged and start thinking, "What a bunch of nasty jerks. They won't even let me get my coffee or say goodbye to my colleagues and friends. I gave them 10 years of my dedicated blood and sweat and just yesterday I stayed late to make sure the 'critical job' was done. Now they put me out like a piece of garbage! I am kicked out to the curb and left totally exposed to the elements. I feel raw and naked. I feel humiliated and worthless. What the hell am I going to do?"

A Big Dose of Self-Pity, Then Dust Off the Ol' Resume and Get Cracking

You know who I am talking about. Yes, you! You are the big, tough, grown men and women who look and act like Grizzly Adams (okay, maybe not the women!) that burst into tears when speaking with me on the phone, and then hang up. Eventually you call back really angry, then you call back really depressed and ask for job search advice. I give you tips and strategies that are proven to work in a real-life laboratory. You hear but you do not listen. You say you want to try it the "Internet way" and you say, "I know how to do this.

I have a resume, I know about the job boards, and I have contacts." So off you go with what you think is the new "get a job by the Internet" thing—the "click and send" method of sending your resume to as many jobs as you can find on the Web, as well as sending your resume to your contacts.

You think to yourself, "Wow! It's so easy. Isn't technology great?" and you start plastering your resume to adverts on the Internet using the old "click and send" technique. You get lucky and you get an interview. You are happy. Then you remember INTERVIEW—and you think, "Holy heart failure, Batman."

Let's face it: Interviews are stressful, especially if you are not prepared! You will have to share your faults and weaknesses with someone you only met 10 minutes ago. It is akin to being stripped down naked in front of a stranger.

This is usually how the interview unwinds: The interviewers' faces are expressionless, and they look at their watches incessantly. They ask you very insightful questions, such as "If you were a vegetable, which vegetable would you be?" You really want to answer, "I would be a real big frozen carrot so I could stick it up your you-know-what, buddy!" Instead, you answer meekly, as they write furiously with their eyes bulging, hemming and hawing and hanging on every word. You think to yourself, "They are acting like I am revealing the secrets to Tesla's Death Ray." You answer, "To tell you the truth, I have never, ever thought about it." You wonder if this is the right answer, as you now start sweating. Vegetable—what vegetable? You are told the standard: They will get back to you next week. As you walk to your car you think, "All those interview books I read didn't have anything on being a vegetable. Go figure. What vegetable?"

REJECTION

Once you recover from the interview ordeal, the waiting starts. You sit around waiting on pins and needles, hoping to get a call back. Every time the phone rings, you jump out of your skin. The call does come, not after a week, but after three weeks, with the following news: "Thank you. We really liked you but we hired someone that meets our needs better."

You interpret their message to mean, "Thanks for coming in, but we don't hire unemployed losers who cannot figure out which vegetable they are." Your confidence gets ratcheted down one extra notch.

You think your "click and send" approach worked. Why abandon it now? You keep plugging away, with diminishing returns, exemplified by your dwindling bank account and level of confidence. Many of you have been at this "click and send," one-armed-bandit game for months, some even for years, with nothing to show for your efforts.

You say, "Okay, Paul, you nailed me! Thanks for making me relive those moments. What's your point?" You need a new game plan. The problem is you are taking an old playbook into a new fight. Job search has changed. Advances in technology make the way jobs are found and filled online distinctly different from just a few years ago. Before you move on you must first adjust your attitude or you will continue to fail miserably.

GET REPROGRAMMED EFFORTLESSLY USING REVOLUTIONARY TECHNOLOGY

In counseling professionals who are involved in changing jobs, I have observed that a continuous lack of progress and repeated rejection lead to a massive loss of confidence. As if an unemployed professional does not have enough to contend with already, employers admit to favoring employed candidates. Being unemployed carries a stigma. Newell Rubbermaid's Mike Rickheim said, "The best candidate in a hiring manager's eyes is the one who doesn't have to make a move. They are and have been gainfully employed and there is another employer who really wants to keep them...."[2]

Your interpretation is that all the events are piling up and pointing to the deck being stacked against you. You are convinced that losing your job hurts, even though it is one you did not like. The anxiety builds and builds until it is palpable.

For many of you, your last job was not even a job you could really claim to like, yet you are still very upset about losing a less-than-ideal job. Why? Because you believe losing your job is a reflection on you as a person—that your job is your identity; it is who you are. You measure your worth based on being employed and the job you do. By giving all your personal power and identity to your employer, you end up feeling powerless and helpless when you lose your job. If this is the situation you find yourself in now, you need to change your attitude, and quickly. But how? You have read all the self-help books, you have tried the self-help stuff, but still you are back where you started. Get ready for something totally different.

I have spent years studying the self-help and motivational gurus; the message they give you is to change your language and be positive, and this will change your attitude and result in changing your outcome. In other words, by changing your language and your attitude you change what you focus on and attract. My experience has shown that you can pump someone up with all these techniques, but left to their own devices and without constant repetitive coaching or very rigorous self-disciplined self-talk, the professionals I have coached fall back into self-defeating and limiting self-talk patterns very quickly. If you agree with this simple statement, "What you say to yourself controls the way you feel and how you feel controls the way you act," then it is imperative to find a way to adjust the way you feel about yourself that does not require a destructive behavior like alcohol, drugs, or food, or takes a lot of money, time, or effort.

I went in a relentless search for something better, and I found it. I discovered that applying the best peak performance technology to job search works. How do I know? I have found that it has changed my life positively and the professionals I coach swear by it also. The criteria that I set were to find a technology that was easy to implement, and required very little money and virtually no effort. "No effort" was a must, because what I found in coaching is that people/professionals want to change but they do not want to be uncomfortable. In other words, if there is any pain involved in changing, most professionals will not stick with it. What I am about to reveal may be for some the most important discovery in this book and the most life-changing discovery they will ever make.

Throughout the last few years I have been prescribing this revolutionary technology to my clients with outstanding results. As I said, job loss can have tremendous negative effects on one's psyche, to the point of very tragic outcomes, and this technology has proven to be a godsend for my clients. What is it, you ask?

It is brainwave therapy! It is the simplest, most affordable way I have found to tap into your higher potential and unleash your power to think, create, and heal, and at the same time bring about real, lasting change. When I say affordable, I mean it. It costs only a *one-time* investment of about $10 to get great results. That is all you need to invest—really! The great thing about brainwave technology is there's no training necessary and no big learning curve, no sweat, no effort—and you don't need to spend tons of money or buy expensive equipment. It is really simple and revolutionary—almost sounds too good to be true, right? Well, let me tell you: I was skeptical at first, but I have seen it work time and time again, and it only takes 30 minutes a day.

This is how easy it is: Find a quiet place, sit down or lie down, and listen to your iPod or MP3 player to bring about massive positive change. I know what you are thinking: All the money you have spent has gone to waste since now you can throw away thousands of dollars' worth of books and tapes, stop going to those self-help conferences, and instead spend 30 minutes a day chilling and relaxing. Without getting into the medical research in depth, it is all about balancing your brain. A balanced brain enhances your ability to think, learn, create, and recall. Your perception expands, your memory improves, and you can focus more easily, which leads to much better sleep and makes you much more resilient to stress. More importantly, the brainwave enhancement brings freedom from fear, worry, and even addictions that have stood in the way of getting what you want out of life, including the job you really want, as well as experiencing more fulfilment and joy. The professionals I have turned on to brainwave technology tell me they feel better and do better when taking on new challenges, especially, they say, when faced with stressful situations such as those experienced in job search: talking to strangers, selling themselves, going on interviews, and when asking for a higher salary than they normally would. Most importantly, they tell me that they believe it gave them confidence, the ability to visualize exactly what they wanted, and the energy they needed to land their new job. I know it works for me, and through my practice I know it works for others.

The science behind brainwave therapy was first discovered by biophysicist Gerald Oster at Mount Sinai Hospital in New York City. What is it? It is really quite simple, from the user's standpoint. Brainwave therapy sends pure, precisely tuned sound waves of different frequencies to your brain via stereo headphones. His research showed that by regulating what sounds are sent to each ear, a "binaural beat" is interpreted by the brain. These precisely tuned sound frequencies delivered to the brain through headphones drive brain activity into high-level states of mind. The type of sound wave delivered engenders different brain states known as:

➤ Alpha for heightened creativity and deep relaxation

➤ Beta for high focus and concentration

➤ Theta for meditation, insight, and memory

➤ Delta for deep sleep and healing

➤ Gamma to increase cognition and improve IQ

Scientists discovered that within minutes of listening, the sound frequencies start to balance the left and right hemispheres of your brain. This balancing creates a remarkable state called *hemispheric synchronization*. This hemispheric synchronization drives the electrical activity of your brain into powerful states that are normally unattainable. Scientists have noted that this rare phenomenon was accompanied by flashes of creative insight, euphoria, intensely focused concentration, deep calm, and enhanced learning abilities. These are the states I want you to tap into by changing your internal programming so you can get on track to getting the job you really want. This technology is clinically proven to work.

This technology is often called *guided meditation.* The problem with traditional meditation, from what I have studied, is there is a big learning curve, and it does not work for everyone; brainwave technology, on the other hand, has no learning curve, and you do not have to learn how to get "in state." All you have to do is be receptive and let the technology put you in state. Simply let it happen. I have not met one person who has tried it and said it did not work for him or her.

Want more evidence that it works? Here are some great endorsements from clinical and medical professionals:

> "After only 18 minutes of meditating with Brain Sync, we've seen patients reach deep levels of meditation that would normally take 18 years of practice to attain." —Drew Pierson, PhD, biofeedback researcher[3]

> "These programs are extremely powerful tools for producing peak performance brain states." —Michael Hutchison, author of *Megabrain: New Tools and Techniques for Brain Growth and Mind Expansion*[4]

> "…the audio technology that was instrumental to the success of my work with smokers, and work with all types of addiction and disease."—Edward A. Taub, MD, spokesperson for the American Medical Association's national Stop Smoking Campaign[5]

My team and I are working on an "Interview to Win" guided meditation that will eventually be available to the public.

I recommend that you take advantage of this technology right away. Go to *www.transitiontohired.com/resources,* start with downloading the audio program labeled "Must-Have Brain Wave Therapy," and experience for yourself what I and my clients have been benefiting from for years. Remember: The great thing is it is really effortless and has tremendous lasting impact.

ALTERNATIVE APPROACH

If you are a pessimist by nature and you do not want to change your life with brainwave technology then you must realize that it will be much harder for you to find work. Why? Most employers I know do not want to hire a sour puss. If you want to get hired, make sure to practice changing your self-talk to positive self-talk; this way you will change your attitude. To learn how to do this, an alternative resource for you is the book *Learned Optimism: How to Change Your Mind and Your Life* by Martin Seligman (Vintage Books, 1992). It offers many proven techniques to get you on the right track.

Now that you have another critically important tool to take on the challenges of job search, it is time to figure out what you want and what advantages you have to offer.

CHAPTER 2

WHO ARE YOU?

"KNOW THYSELF."
—SOCRATES[1]

WORK AND YOUR LEGACY

Self-awareness is power when it comes to planning your work life or career. In other words, really knowing who you are is power in discovering which jobs or careers are best for you. Ideally, it is about finding what fits for you, rather than trying to fit in.

Why is having the "right" job or career important? When you are in the "right" job, you are in the best position to maximize your strengths, and make the biggest professional or work-related impact.

The impact you make leaves a trail, and this trail is your legacy. Your legacy is the proof that you have contributed. This contribution, or this legacy, affects your feeling of fulfillment, and ideally you want to be as fulfilled as possible. If you feel unfulfilled, your trail is most likely leading to nowhere, which undoubtedly is causing frustration for you. Your trail may have been leading somewhere at some point, but now has been redirected. This redirection may be caused by change, and change comes in many different forms. You need to adjust to this change and get the direction straightened out first in order to achieve fulfillment. The best way to get back on track is to find a reference point to start from.

The first step is to identify who you are and what makes you tick. With this knowledge, as you will soon discover, you can then target the best job or career for you. Employed, unemployed, or in transition, by choice or by force, the key to getting the job you want or to figuring out what job you want is to know who you are.

ARE YOU PREPARED FOR A JOB OR CAREER CHANGE?

Driven by agents of change, the world is transforming rapidly. These transformations and paradigm shifts affect us all. Consider the speed of change in portable devices, including media players and mobile devices. A big shift in thinking occurred from thinking of media devices as individual, one-function devices, to these incredibly integrated miniature multi-functional mobile devices. This is an area of technology that has seen some amazing progress in my lifetime, from the beginnings, with the invention of the stereo belt in 1972, to these smart mobile phones with Internet, e-mail, and text, as well as rich media such as camera, audio player, audio recorder, video player, TV, and video recorder capabilities as standard features. You can even bank, buy groceries or pharmaceuticals, and send money from one mobile device to another.

Constant change just like portable/mobile technology is occurring across all areas of our lives, forcing changes in our careers, and career directions. The skills you relied on for the last 10 years were valuable, and now they are, or may be, obsolete. You need to keep your skills up with new technology and processes or you risk losing your edge in the battle for jobs. You can have the greatest job skills in the world, but if no one knows you have them or can't find you to offer you a job, then those skills go to waste. Just as importantly, you need to know how to communicate that you have these important skills and be able to market yourself so you can attract the right attention from the right employers. Alternatively, you may simply choose to adjust your career or your job focus to better reflect your current skills and interests. Because over time you change and develop new skills, knowledge, and interests, you may reach a point where you want a new challenge. If this is the case, you may choose to examine what new avenues are open to you that meet your new skills and interests. In a fast-shifting world a professional needs to be nimble and quick to adjust to take advantage of interesting opportunities as one door closes and others open. The bottom line is: There will always be opportunities, but will you be ready for those opportunities?

Many of you may feel comfortable, and oblivious to a tsunami of change that may affect you. These agents of change come in many forms. For example, a shocking life event, disease, a death of someone close, a revelation, a loss of a long-time job, or a mid-life crisis can force you to change. Nothing will stimulate the urge for self-awareness more than a full-blown disruption of life. For all these reasons, you need to be prepared and have the tools at your disposal—and know how to use these tools—to find work or to have work find you.

If you are employed, be proactive and take advantage of this chapter to discover your skills, knowledge, and style as well as your interest and what drives you. This most likely has changed significantly from your first job to now. If, on the other hand, change has been forced upon you, take the time to reevaluate and discover who you are before seeking a new job or committing to a new job.

How Formative Programming Influences Career/Job Choices

Consider that many of you did not get supportive messages growing up, and many of you got mixed messages when it came to choosing work or a career. Some of you were bombarded by statements like, "You will never amount to anything," "You're stupid," "Why can't you ever do anything right?" or "You need to get real and think about a real job, not this pie-in-the-sky stuff." Regardless of the message you received or interpreted, you made it this far, and if you are an adult you have the ability to choose, so take the opportunity to actually make a new choice as you work through this chapter. Remember: Your past does not equal your future.

For many of you it was implied that you should do what is/was sensible and predictable instead of pursuing a dream that will/would fulfill you. For example, some of you became doctors, lawyers, engineers, teachers, scientists, chemists, or professionals of some kind. Some of you let life push and pull you into a career and, as though on auto pilot, the terms of your careers were dictated for you. Others of you have floated from job to job with no sense of purpose, or have found it hard to retain a job.

Some of you may have received very supportive messages from your parents, but were led astray by peer pressure or other influential people in your life who conveyed negative messages about the dreams you shared with them. You started second-guessing your dreams. You became fearful and started believing you were not good enough, pretty enough, strong enough, tall enough, smart enough, or whatever else enough, to go after your dreams. Eventually you broke down and followed the path your parents wanted for you, or a path that provided food and shelter and allowed you to be *normal,* get married, have 1.2 children, and take 0.73 trips per year—the path of least resistance.

Many of you have received great fulfillment until now from your careers, regardless of the message or path you took, but now you feel something has changed, you have changed, or something is missing and you don't know what to do next because you don't know who you are and what your capabilities truly are. In other words, it has been a long time since you evaluated yourself. You have not taken the time to do an inventory of your interests, skills, and competencies. It has been my experience that most professionals would prefer to grate their fingers on a cheese grater (ouch!) than sit down and do a thorough personal inventory.

INNER CONFLICT

Perhaps the wrong job or career choice is leaving you unfulfilled. Feeling unfulfilled leads to inner conflict, and it builds as you watch your life pass you by. If you do not deal with it, one day this inner conflict will surface, and manifest itself through frustration with your identity and/or your career or job. You may be frustrated with the path your life has been taking, and the path that lies ahead. What you thought was the easy and sensible thing to do with your life turns out to be the thing that has you sinking in the quicksand of despair.

Faced with this discomfort, some deal with it by pseudo-medicating with prescription drugs, or medicating with illicit drugs, alcohol, or other destructive behaviors.

Others just grin and bear it, believing this is their lot in life. You say to yourself, "What can I do now?" or "I am too old," or "I do not have the education or the smarts to change." Or you may kid yourself and say, "I am content."

Are you really?

Are you living your dream?

If you choose to stay on the same path, you will eventually retire, shop at warehouse outlet malls throughout the southern United States, buy a Snuggie from a shopping channel and a warehouse pack of Preparation H per year from Costco, then die. If you recognize the frustration for what it is and you actually decide to do something about it before it becomes a crisis, you are truly blessed.

As mentioned earlier, perhaps a job termination, a break-up, or a tragedy triggers full-blown frustration. Maybe a simple question you ask yourself can be the trigger, such as, "Why do I do this, day in and day out?" or "Why do I live an ant's life?" Get up, scurry around getting ready for work, line up in traffic jams, line up to park or line up to get on the subway. Scurry to line up to get coffee and then scurry around at work, just to line up again for lunch and after work for the subway home. Get home exhausted, fall asleep, and dream about whether you are the next one in line for a promotion or the next one in line to get fired. Just before you wake you dream about how your next thrill will be lining up your bills in the evening so you can pay them. You get to wake up and start all over again. Yeah! Is this the way to live? There has to be a better way.

The Importance of Passion

Discovering your passion is critical to putting your passion to work. In order to discover your passion you need to be aware of or discover your interests and driving forces. Passion is the combination of your interests and driving forces (the things that motivate you). When you choose work that you are passionate about, and that matches well with your competence, you set off a transformation: Your work is not work anymore; it's what you do to get your kicks.

How do you discover what you are passionate about? By answering these questions for yourself:

- What are my interests?
- What are my driving forces?

Interests

When it comes to choosing work one of the chief complaints I hear is this: "I don't know what I am interested in." In the following sections you will uncover your interests.

What Are Your Interests?

The goal is to uncover what fascinates and intrigues you. What interests you? Ultimately, if you can find what interests you, and incorporate those interests into a job or career, you have a key piece of the puzzle figured out.

A Primer: Review Your Past for clues

Take the time to remember when you were a kid. What did you want to be when you grew up? What jobs interest you now? Did you follow that career path? If you did, do you still like it? Perhaps you did, and felt fulfilled for many years, and now it's time for a change.

What other jobs or careers appeal to you? What parts of the job or career were fun?

Look over your work life:

- Enumerate your accomplishments. Include some volunteer accomplishments or coaching sports teams. Don't be shy; fill up 30 pages if you want to. Now you should feel better when you review your list. In many cases you should be amazed at what you have achieved. What accomplishments from this list gave you a sense of pride and success? This will tell you what is important to you.
- Go over the people you worked with in your mind. Write down answers to the following: Whom did you like working with? Whom did you hate? What bosses did you like and what were their styles? This will give you insight into the type of people you like to work with, or the type of manager you get along with. What was the work environment like? Was it structured? Was it fly-by-the-seat-of-your-pants? Was it slow-paced or fast-paced? Was there lots of people interaction or none? What type of environment did you like most, and why?

You now have, through this primer, a cursory understanding of what your dreams were, what type of work might interest you, the type of people you like to work with, and the work environment you like. If you did not get much from this exercise, hang in there.

You now need to dig much deeper.

Interest Discovery Made Easy With O*Net

It is well worth it to get a more in-depth profile of your interests, for free from O*Net OnLine (*www.onetonline.org*). O*NET OnLine was created for the U.S. Department of Labor. By following through you will indicate your liking for 180 job-related activities. Your answers will then be put into "Holland" scores reflecting the preferences for careers described as Realistic, Investigative, Artistic, Social, Enterprising, and Conventional (RIASEC). Dr. Holland's research demonstrated that people and jobs can be described in Holland scores or RIASEC scores. The occupations in the O*Net database are organized into RIASEC categories, so scores from the O*Net Interest Profiler can be easily matched to careers worthy of exploration. You can download the O*Net Interest Profiler software at *www.transitiontohired.com/resources*.

Pick-and-Choose Exercise

I highly recommend that you use the O*Net Interest Profiler, but I know some of you will never get around to it. Alternatively, put a check mark beside the things that are of interest to you in Table 2.1 (on the next page). Add to this list by jotting down all your interests, above and beyond this list. Jot down everything that comes to mind: dressmaking, windmills, poultry, horticulture, erotica, you name it—get it down.

TABLE 2.1: INTERESTS

Accounting	Acting	Alternative Medicine	Antiques
Archeology	Art	Astronomy	Automobiles
Biology	Birding	Boating	Betting
Carpentry	Catering	Chemistry	Children
Coaching	Community	Communications	Computers
Conservation	Counseling	Criminology	Dancing
Designing	E-commerce	Education	Environment
Ethics	Falconry	Fashion	Finances
Fishing	Fitness	Flying	Forensics
Franchising	Gardening	Geriatric Care	Golf
Gourmet Foods	Graphic Design	Health	Horticulture
Home Renovation	Hospitality	Human Resources	Human Rights
IT	Interior Decorating	Investing	Journalism
Kite Flying	Landscaping	Languages	Law
Lecturing	Literature	Marketing	Martial Arts
Massage	Media	Mentoring	Origami
Orgasms	Ornithology	Painting	Philosophy
Photography	Physics	Poetry	Politics
Process Research	Product Design	Psychology	Pandas
Quality Control	Quality Assurance	Research	Real Estate
Religion	Retail	Road Design	Sales
Security	Seniors' Issues	Sex Therapy	Small Business
Spirituality	Sports	Stock Market	Teaching
Temporary Work	Tennis	Translation	Travel
United Way	Volunteering	Websites	Wilderness
Wool	Writing	Yoga	Xenogamy

Adapted from ADV Advanced Technical Services Inc. Candidate Profiler. [2]

Elicit a Theme or Category of Work

Now that you have a good list, see if you can group the list into categories or themes to uncover your work interests. If you have not done so yet and you believe you have a great grasp of your RIASEC Interest Area or score, and you prefer to scan the list of occupations classified by major interest area, then you can get a comprehensive list at *www.transitiontohired.com/resources.*

Is there a predominant theme? Are there any jobs or careers that are available or that you can create that would match the theme? Is the theme a job interest or a hobby interest? Make the distinction by asking yourself, "Would I like to have this theme as the predominant factor in my work?" Even if you are using the RIASEC results from the profiler, the occupations that show up in the different categories may point you to a different interest or occupation that is not on the O*Net list. Be open and think beyond the list. For instance, at the time of writing this book, "social media coordinator" was not listed as an occupation on the O*Net list.

Let's say you chose biology, boating, criminology, forensics, falconry, gardening, law, ornithology, security, and wilderness from Table 2.1. Upon review of these interests, a matching job or occupation that would meet most of these interests is not apparent. However, did you consider a conservation officer? As you can now see, this would meet most of the interests chosen and would most likely touch on all these interests. Do the same with your list and review the RIASEC results to see what other inspiring occupations you can discover or even create, or which occupations from the O*Net list excite you. Jot down all the possibilities that appeal to you.

DRIVING FORCES

The other component of passion is your driving forces. Your values have a corresponding driving force. Your values are molded by upbringing, role model(s), heroes, experiences, and your inner compass. A value is a concept that describes the beliefs you have. The sum total of your values forms your personal blueprint. The blueprint, formed by your values, is the map that guides you. When your blueprint is aligned with your actions, you feel comfortable and together. When your compass is scrambled and it leads you off course or away from your blueprint, you start to manifest behaviors that are not empowering. A few behaviors exhibited could be anger, anxiety, irritability, depression, and despondency. When you are aligned you demonstrate positive behaviors, such as enthusiasm, humor, consideration, charm, pragmatism, and ambition, among others.

Your values are the *motivators* that drive you; these are your *driving* forces. If your work is not aligned with your driving forces, you are very likely miserable. Here are a few examples so you can get a better understanding of driving forces being misaligned with one's work.

If one's dominant driving force is to make a lot of money and that person's prime source of income is working at a volunteer-based association, he will be in conflict with his blueprint or inner compass and most likely be miserable.

If one's blueprint included being programmed with "thou shall not kill" and this person is recruited by Tony Soprano to be a hit woman, this person has a problem. She will be terrible at her job, and most likely the outcome for her would be to eventually be dressed up by Tony's henchmen with cement boots, and be invited by Tony to visit the "fishies" in the Hudson River.

TABLE 2.2: DRIVING FORCES

Value	Drives You Toward
Traditional	Order/Organization/Planning
Theoretical	Knowledge/Learning
Social	Helping/Assisting
Individualistic	Power
Utilitarian	Money
Aesthetic	Beauty/Harmony

Created from concept from TTI Performance Systems Ltd.[3]

6 Basic Values—And What These Drive Us Toward

We all have some degree of each value in our makeup. This means if we measure our values on a gradient scale by, say, using a test for this purpose, we will score in one of three areas: near, above, or below the population norm for each value considered. The extent to which we are above or below the norm on a particular value determines how dominant that corresponding driving force is for us. For example, if someone has a high Utilitarian score, money is very important to him. If he has a low score, it is unimportant.

Your driving forces are not easily uncovered; I suggest relying on testing to help you out. Go to *www.transitiontohired.com/resources* to find information on assessments including a free Driving Force Assessment.

Driving Forces

➜ Having a strong *Traditional value* means a strong drive for systems and regulations, rules, laws, and codes of conduct for living.

➜ Having a strong *Theoretical value* means to learn, to be curious, and to be intellectual.

➜ Having a strong *Social value* means you love people, you are kind, you are unselfish, and you like to help others.

➜ Having a strong *Individualistic value* means you like to use your power to influence others.

➜ Having a strong *Utilitarian value* means a passion to gain return on investment of time, resources, and money.

➜ Having a strong *Aesthetic value* means you get delight from the beauty in life, the beauty in life's processes, and the harmony and the grace in the flow of life's events.

YOUR PASSION

The combination of your driving forces and your interests determines your passion. In other words, make sure that the occupation you choose from your O*Net work matches up with your values/driving forces. This is where in my experience I see the biggest mismatch. Everyone concentrates on their interests and do not consider their values and driving forces. By doing this they end up choosing a job that makes them miserable. Here is an example. I had a client who was an immigration lawyer working for the government on a refugee board. His job was to deny entry to people to his country. His strongest value was Social. Because he fell into the job after graduating and it paid well, he did the job for 20 years and was miserable until he coached with me. I pointed out that his values were not lined up with the job he was doing. It did not mean quitting as a lawyer; rather, it meant switching sides, to where he would represent the immigrants and help them get citizenship. This was a life-changing realization for him. Are you in a similar situation? You may love the skills you use in your job but are just doing the job from the wrong side of the fence. (Tell us what you have uncovered. Share it with us at *www.transitiontohired. com/resources.*)

YOUR COMPETENCE: YOUR SKILLS, KNOWLEDGE, AND STYLE

In order to get hired in a job you want, you need to feel confident that you have the potential ability or capability to perform. Your fit for a job is no longer measured by your strengths and weaknesses. Your fit is measured by how your skills, knowledge, style, and behavior match up with the performance standards established for the position you want. These performance standards are often called competencies. (Competencies are described in great detail in Chapter 6.)

Having a passion and getting hired in a job you are passionate about are two very distinct things. You have to be able to express your passion and skills for a particular job or occupation to an employer in his language. In other words, you must be able to demonstrate your passion, as well as demonstrate you have the skills, knowledge, and style required to do the job at an acceptable level. It is imperative, therefore, that you do an inventory of your skills, knowledge, and style.

The sum total of your skills, knowledge, and style is your competence.

COMPETENCE

Your competence is your potential ability or capability to perform. Knowing this comes in very handy not only in terms of career progression but also when transitioning from one industry to another, or from one occupation to another. It should also be noted that competency development is a lifelong progression of doing, experiencing, and thinking. In other words, building your competence is a lifelong pursuit.

How do you determine your competence? By getting the answers to the following empowering questions:

➤ What are my skills?

➤ What knowledge do I have?

➤ What are my distinct operating styles?

Take the time to write down your answers to each of the questions by using the following guidance.

What Are My Skills?

This refers to professional or work skills. Write a list of your skills. Include in this list your education and certifications, as well as your technical skills. This includes qualification or experience in any processes, systems, or programs. Do the same for your functional skills.

Two examples of functional skills for an administrative assistant would be word processing and knowledge of MS office applications. For a chemist they would be use of HPLC systems, method development, and so forth.

What Knowledge Do I Have?

Your knowledge is different from your professional job skills and education. It encompasses everything: information you have gathered; understanding of cultures, languages, challenges, activities, places, ideas; anything else you can think of that may be remotely valuable. It includes special knowledge of industries, competitive knowledge, product positioning, ability to call on your network for help, and ability as a speaker, presenter, or trainer. Remember— anything you can think of.

What Are My Distinct Operating Styles?

Characteristics and behavioral styles are brought to your work, as well as your style of interaction with others at work. You will know your dominant characteristics, whereas others may be difficult to assess. In general these behavior traits are difficult to assess on your own. A good strategy is to take a behavioral assessment. You can find a good behavioral assessment at *www.transitiontohired.com/resources.*

Some examples of behaviors are: assertive, self-confident, entrepreneurial. Independent, venturesome, risk-oriented, competitive. Direct, blunt, authoritative, skeptical, reserved. Analytical, technical, task-oriented. Impatient, sense of urgency, thrive on change. Results- and goal-oriented, hard driver. Driver for achievement, work-oriented, bottom-line oriented. Generalist, multitasker, need variety. Disciplined thinker, very logical decision-making, analysis-paralysis, procrastination, sociable, patient, dependence, low emotional control. Add as many behaviors as you see fit to your list.

Your Styles

Your style encompasses work style, thinking style, stamina/toughness, communication style, supervisee style, and supervisory/management style.

- ➜ Work style: Are you flexible, rigid, goal-oriented, planner, team player, wishy-washy, decisive, perfectionist, generalist, scattered, ambiguous, direct, confrontational, accommodating?

- ➜ Thinking style: How do you solve issues and problems? Are you optimistic, pessimistic, realistic, strategic, analytical, instinctive, perceptive, steadfast, visionary, creative, or focused?

➨ Stamina/toughness: Are you able to take the heat, work under pressure, and work for long hours? Are you an explosive streak worker or consistent plodder, achiever? Pessimistic or optimistic? Can you deal with physical exertion, loud environments, or lots of distraction?

➨ Communication style: Are you direct, influential/persuasive, reserved, enthusiastic, humorous, slow to answer/a thinker?

➨ Supervisee style: How do you like to be supervised or managed? Micro or macro, structured, detailed, told what to do? Are you loyal or a rebel?

➨ Supervisory/management style: Are you democratic/inclusive or dictator, micro or macro, figure it out yourself or step by step, risk-taker or cautious, rule-breaker, or toe the line?

Matching Competence and Interests

Once you have gone through the previous exercise, evaluate your list with the list of occupations you selected previously. Do your interests and competence match up well? If not, then in what areas can you improve or gain the necessary skills? Would taking courses or going to school be a solution in order to pursue an occupation of interest? Often our skills determine what we are interested in. Does your competence elicit new occupations or interests? If nothing comes shining through just yet, that is fine. Clarity will come when you combine your passion, interests, and driving forces with your competence to describe your Sustainable Competitive Advantage.

SUSTAINABLE COMPETITIVE ADVANTAGE (SCA)

How do you combine everything you have learned about yourself, your interests and driving forces, and your skills, knowledge, and style so that it becomes an advantage in your job search? You do this by defining your Sustainable Competitive Advantage (SCA).

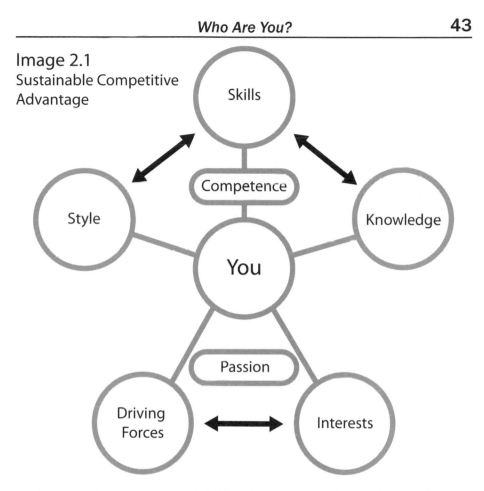

Image 2.1
Sustainable Competitive
Advantage

You may have encountered SCA referred to as a Unique Selling Proposition (USP) or your competitive advantage. The key word here is *sustainable.* In other words, it is part of your core; it is built on your competence and the things that excite you—your passion. Your SCA is resilient no matter the situation you are in.

When you combine your competence, defined by your skills, knowledge, and style, and your passion, defined by your interests and driving forces, you have discovered your Sustainable Competitive Advantage. Once you have a detailed understanding and grasp of your SCA, you are way ahead of your competition, because you know what you are good at, what you are not good at, what you are capable of, what excites you, and what drives you.

Your SCA is what makes *you* uniquely *special.* Armed with your clearly defined SCA, you can target the ideal job you want with passion and confidence. Take a sheet of paper and make a visual representation of your SCA, as in

Image 2.1. Make it big enough so you can enter the predominant attributes for each circle.

Now that you have a good grasp of your SCA, it is time to articulate it and give it a voice by summarizing it into a few paragraphs.

Here is an SCA summary as an example:

I'm a successful entrepreneur with extensive experience in the international recruitment business, supported by the fact that I have won many awards for outstanding achievement in this field. I am a coach who has trained and mentored many to achieve success in business. I am a burgeoning writer with a zany style, and I am extremely passionate about writing. I am a dominant leader of leaders, with great vision and the power of great influence over others. I am at my best when faced with troubleshooting or finding solutions to problems by using my well-developed strategic thinking style and my instinctual ability to predict upcoming events. I am extremely creative and have a wild imagination that gives me a gift for innovation. Management is of negligible interest to me, but when the situation requires I am a macro manager who empowers people to take risks and to learn by doing. One of my challenges is I am not good with detail. As a leader I am confident in the face of adversity, and I get my followers to "loosen up" by making the work environment fun. What I espouse and live by: "You can do anything you want to do. All you have to do is do it, and the money will come."

In Chapter 6 you will learn how to incorporate your SCA into your resume. It is very important that you complete this exercise.

Now that you are armed with your SCA, do any additional occupations or ways to make a living come to mind? Make sure you consider jobs, careers, or opening a new business that matches your SCA.

THE ULTIMATE MOTIVATOR: YOUR *WHY*

As you can see, having the competence to do a specific job does not mean you will be passionate or happy doing that job. You need to be interested in and be driven to do the job, or your values must be well matched to the job or career you choose. **In order for you to excel at a job, you must be capable of doing it and you must be passionate about it.** You do not need to make any concrete decisions just yet on what you are going to pursue in an occupation or your dream job, but knowing why you want to make the effort to find a better job or satisfy your dreams is critical. First ask yourself: Am I willing to make the effort?

What Is Your *WHY?*

If you feel as though it all sounds like too much work, and you have just glossed over everything up to now and you have not really put your heart into it, there is a reason why. This exercise will turn things around for you. Answering "What is my *WHY?*" will get you unstuck and motivated to follow through. Your *WHY* must be big enough to power your will. Will is the product of your *WHY*; it is your best friend—your wing man that gives you the strength to follow through and get the job that is right for you. If your *WHY* is not motivating you, you need to find a bigger *WHY*. Your *WHY* is a combination of all the:

➨ People you love (your family, children, friends)

➨ Things you want to do

➨ Places you want to go to or travel to

➨ Things you want to achieve

➨ Causes you support

➨ Impact you want to leave

What your *WHY* is not, is money; rather, it is the end result of what you want to do with your money.

If you would like to bring your *WHY* to life and create your *WHY* video, go to *www.transitiontohired.com/resources* to learn more.

PART II

CONFIDENCE

CHAPTER 3

THE POWER OF WISHES, DREAMS, AND GOALS

"TO ACCOMPLISH GREAT THINGS, WE MUST NOT ONLY ACT, BUT ALSO DREAM;
NOT ONLY PLAN, BUT ALSO BELIEVE."
—ANATOLE FRANCE[1]

Why are wishes, dreams, and goals so important to your job search and getting the job you want? Before you find out how to get somewhere, you need to know where you are going. Then you can figure out how to get there. You may know your competence and passion as well as which occupations interest you and why it is important for you to move forward, but how do you know exactly which job you want, and, what level, or what your progression should be? You need a plan.

Most people don't get what they want because they don't *know* what they want. Wishes, dreams, and goals work together to define what you want and how to get it. Many people have trouble with the concept of goal setting.

➥ When you set goals, are you actually setting goals, or are these wishes, desires, or dreams?

➥ Why bother with goal setting?

➥ Are there advantages to goal setting?

➥ How do you tap into your dreams in order to set new goals in terms of a job, a new career, or a work-related achievement?

➥ What do wishes, dreams, and goals have to do with confidence?

Let's get started answering some of these questions by first meeting Eva.

EVA AND "THE ANSWER"

I worked at a country fair when I was 14 years old in a town called Merrickville, where my parents owned a hobby farm. We did not have a vacation home or a cottage. My dad believed in physical work as a hobby, and I spent some great summers at the farm, working, fishing, and farming.

My job at the fair was to run the cat game and the basket game. The cat game was where you threw three hard balls at stuffed leather cats with heavy bases, and had to knock three cats off the fence to win a prize. (If that game still exists, here is how you beat it: If you throw a ball at their heads, the ball just whizzes through and the cat stays put. If you aim at the cats' bases, off they tumble from the fence.)

In the basket game, you threw three softballs at a slanted fruit bushel basket. If you could get all three balls to stay in the basket you won a prize. Even if you took care to toss the ball at the basket gently, the ball would hit the bottom of the basket and it would rebound out. The trick was to spin the ball as you threw it into the basket, in such a way that the ball would wheel around the sides of the basket, and settle down slowly and gently into the bottom.

Why did I tell you about these super games? Just to show you young ones how exciting our games were, and how much fun we had compared to those boring video games you play. Plus, at night I got to hang around after the fair closed to be around the carnie people, sit around a fire, and listen to their tales.

There was a fortune-teller at the fair. Her claim to fame was making what you wanted come true. Her performing name was "Eva the Mystical Fair Maiden." She was obviously quite good. She always had people lined up at her booth. When her clients were about to exit her booth, she would hand them "The Answer," a mysteriously folded, elegant, gold-colored piece of paper about the size of a match box. On it, it was said, was the secret to make one's dreams come true. She would instruct them not to show it to anyone or else their yearning would not be fulfilled.

She was sitting beside me at the fire one night. I asked her what was written inside "The Answer." She said, "If you want to find out, give me two dollars, and promise not to tell anyone what is in 'The Answer' until I am dead and gone." I said, "Really, I have to pay you?!" She said, "Of course, young man. This is my job, the one I am passionate about, and there is no shame in making money from something you love doing. Rather, it is a fabulous thing, so pay up, darling!" I found a $2 bill and gave it to her (yes, in Canada at one time we had orange $2 bills).

She began by dancing and jumping up and down and speaking gibberish in some foreign tongue. It was like she was a different person. Her facial expressions changed, and her voice was hoarse and scary. She told me to close my eyes and just to imagine what I "truly wanted." After a while she said, "Just see what will happen when you get what you want." Then she said, "Think of how getting what you want makes you feel." I focused real hard on following her instructions to see and feel.

She said, "I want you to ponder all the aptitude, talent, skills, power, and all the distinctive capabilities you have." By now she had stopped dancing and she was close enough for me to feel her hot breath on my face, and she finally asked, "Are you ready to move on?" I said, "Yes."

At that point she started dancing and shouting to the sky something I did not understand, and—no kidding—lightning started streaking across the sky right at that moment. I felt shivers run through my body and I felt paralyzed, as if my feet were welded to the ground. I was told later that everyone around the fire was mesmerized, even though they had seen her dance hundreds of times before.

I felt a blast of cold wind across my face, which revived me from my stupor just as she said, "Now, you know what you want and you saw it. You felt the feelings of having it. You know you have the capabilities of getting what you want, so now who is going to help you get what you want? Think of the faces of the people you know who can help you. How will you get them to lend a hand in getting what you want?" She asked me, "Do you have a good grasp of everyone you will need?"

She stopped dancing and chanting, and I heard her sit down and say, "Everything is within you. You know exactly what you want, your interests, your passions, your desires, you know your skills and your capabilities, and you even know who can assist you in getting what you want and how to persuade them to help you get what you want. So now, in your mind, see the first step you have to take to get what you want."

As I was going over all this in my mind with my eyes firmly closed she slipped into my shirt pocket, unbeknown to me, "The Answer."

She said, "Trust in yourself. When you know exactly and clearly what is your first step, open your eyes." I listened carefully to her instructions and when the time was right I opened my eyes. I was disoriented and dizzy, and I asked her where my slip of paper was as I looked down on the ground thinking I may have dropped it. She looked at me with a smile, hugged me, and whispered in my ear, "Trust yourself; you know your first step and therefore 'The Answer' will be revealed." As she walked away I stood there bewildered for a few seconds as I watched her fade slowly into the dark. I ran after her but it was as if she had just disappeared—vanished. I ran around looking for her for five minutes until I was out of breath and then thought, "Wow, all that—what a bummer and no revelation." I said goodbye to the rest of the group around the fire and in unison they gave me reassuring look that I interpreted to mean "You will be okay, kid." I started my long walk home and the clouds must have dissipated because every now and then I could glance up to the sky and see the stars. At one point I looked up and caught a "shooting star," as my mom called it. I closed my eyes, just like my mom had taught me to do on camping trips as a child, and I made the same wish I had made with Eva.

When I opened my eyes I immediately was drawn to my shirt pocket. I reached in and felt the smooth and delicate feel of expensive paper. I teased it out of my pocket like it was the most precious jewel in the world and I cupped it with both hands for fear I may lose it again. I unfolded it with the care of a surgeon, very gently, and with the light from the stars I read "The Answer." A great big grin exploded onto my face as I tucked my answer securely into my pocket. End of story.

I think it's okay to tell you what was written inside "The Answer," because Eva is probably dead and gone by now. However, if I told you right now, it would not be much fun, would it? I guess you will just have to wait a little longer.

YOUR WISH LIST

Wishes are a double-edged sword, because we use the term *wishes* or *desires* to define things that we want or desire but we are *not totally committed* to following through and getting. The negative aspect of wishes is that most people do not use them to define their dreams and their goals, but rather simply keep wishing their whole life away. Making this "non-commitment" distinction allows you to think about things you may want or cherish without having to decide to commit to them, without having to pass moral or social judgment on them, or even without evaluating if you are capable of getting them. This way it frees you up; nothing is excluded, nothing is off limits, and nothing is taboo as you "free think" your wish list.

Here is an exercise that will help discover your wishes. Take out a sheet of paper or two, and for the next five minutes write down anything that comes to mind with respect to the following questions. Keep in mind there are no money, age, or other restrictions—no impediments whatsoever. (Maybe you love your career. If that is the case, what level of position would you like to attain in your career?) Use the following questions to help you get started.

- ➩ If anything were possible, what would you want to do or accomplish in your work?

- ➩ What would you like your work to be? Underwater explorer, gorilla tamer, doctor?

- ➩ What level of position would you like to attain in your career?

- ➩ What would you like to learn?

- ➩ Do you want a new career? What type of career?

- ➩ Is money important to you? How much? What job brings outrageous amounts of money? Be creative.

- ➩ Where do you want to work? The Bahamas, Hawaii, or on the moon?

Remember, there are no money, age, or other restrictions—no impediments whatsoever. Anything, like going to the moon, test-driving Ferraris, being a rain barrel maker, or building upside-down houses is okay. Label the list you just created as your "work wish list."

If you do not have very much on your list, you are in trouble. You have lost your ability to imagine.

Go back and take as long as it takes to get in touch with your imagination again by getting the guided meditation that is recommended in Chapter 1 and actually *listen* to it.

WISHES, DREAMS, AND CONFIDENCE

As previously stated, wishes are a double-edged sword, because we use the term *wishes* or *desires* to define things that we want or desire but we are *not totally committed* to following through and getting. The negative aspect of wishes is that most people do not use them to define their dreams and their goals, but rather simply keep wishing their whole life away. By contrast, a dream is a wish you are *committed* to achieving in the longer term (for example, five-plus years out).

Dreams are "burn the boat" decisions. Burn the boat decisions are committed decisions. Metaphorically speaking, you take a boat from the mainland to an island; when you get to the island you burn the boat; there is no going back. The key word in the dream definition is *committed*. Without commitment there can be no confidence. Once you commit to a dream, you know exactly what you want and you have an unwavering belief that you are going to get it. It might get shaky and scary at times, but you are committed to figuring out how to get it. You are confident that you will get there, because you have your SCA backing you up and an unwavering belief.

When I toyed with the idea to write a book it began as a wish that I pondered for more than seven years. It then became a dream with a five-year plan of execution—three years of work hours in writing and conceiving, and two years of work hours in building a platform and marketing. I had to be totally committed to achieving my dream. I did not know how I was going to write a book, or get an agent or get a publisher, or build a platform and a ProfessionaliBrand. All of that did not matter because I was committed. I knew my SCA and I knew I would succeed.

> When you know your WHY, and you are COMMITTED to your DREAM, and you know WHO YOU ARE then you automatically ALIGN and have the CONFIDENCE and belief that the HOW will reveal itself if you are willing to take the first step and take ACTION.

Your Dream Actualization List

Once you have your wishes from your work wish list you can break these down further into dreams. In my definition dreams are the byproducts of wishes. Dreams are wishes you are committed to achieving within five to 10 years.

Take those wishes from your work wish list and narrow your list down to two wishes you are committed to achieving in five years. Call this one your "dream actualization list."

DREAMS AND GOALS

What is the difference between dreams and goals? The difference between dreams and goals is not so obvious. A goal by definition is simply a well-defined, short-term target, with the key word being *defined*. A dream is a long-term target that is achieved by reaching a number of goals. Dreams are the big picture, whereas goals are the steps you take to reach your dream. Dreams are concrete but they are not as well defined as goals. In order to progress toward attaining your dreams, you need well-defined goals as stepping stones.

You want to climb the right mountain, so you need to understand the concept of dreams. A dream is a long-term target that you are *committed* to achieving, but you are not as limited by the defined nature of goals.

Dreams or long-term goals can seem big, daunting, and even impossible at first blush. The time line can extend from five years to a lifetime. Your goal list, on the other hand, is the map you follow to get you there.

The dream is the ultimate target; it can be flexible, and can be adjusted and refined along the way as you move closer toward its achievement.

Think of it this way: Your wish may be to go on a long, adventuresome automobile trip. Your dream would be to cross the United States—that is, travel from Los Angeles to New York City, by car over two years. Your goals would be securing a car, the stops along the way, the cities, the sites, and the entertainment stops on your way to your destination end point New York City.

To recap, dreams are characterized by what you want and why, whereas goals are the steps, the plan, and the map that gets you there.

Dreams and goals work well together. If you only have dreams without the framework of goals, you can easily get demoralized by the enormity of the dream.

SMART Goals

The short-term target is what we call a SMART goal. It just means that it is well defined and has distinct parameters. SMART means Specific, Measurable, Action-oriented, Realistic/Relevant, and Time-specific. So a SMART goal is a defined short-term target, focused and specific, that is under your control (or you have some control over). Setting SMART goals allows for small steps that are attainable and therefore acts as the facilitator to achievement of the dream.

On the other hand, if you only have goals you can get stuck concentrating so much on the steps that you forget where you are heading. Most importantly, you can become blind to why you are going for the dream in the first place. You might miss opportunities that allow you to jump way ahead because your head is down all the time focusing so hard on the goals. Look up every once in a while and make sure the dream is still something you want and that you are heading in the right direction.

Reviewing your long-term goals or your dream helps you figure out if your strategy and your goals are working, and it allows you to make corrections as needed to stay on track. Accomplishing short-term goal after goal may feel great, but you must ask yourself: "Is it getting me where I want to go?"

The bottom line is goals require much more specific detail than dreams and they are much more short-term, more focused, and specific.

Example

Your Wish: I want to retire when I am 65, having been recognized in my field.

Your Dream: I want to be a director of a lab at Pfizer by the time I am 55 and making the equivalent of $180,000 per year in today's dollars.

Examples of SMART Goals

➜ Send an e-mail to John Smith today and ask him if we can meet once a month on the third Thursday of each month for lunch at Pedro's so he can mentor me on my dream of becoming a director of the laboratory within 10 years.

➜ Based on previous discussions with John, take the plunge, go online, and sign up for the Queen's MBA fall session of 2011.

➜ Send an e-mail to Brad, my director, requesting a meeting and push for MBA sponsorship from the company with a goal of getting a minimum $10,000 per year from them—plus one half-day off per week for study time. If no sponsorship or time off work is given, then work out some flex time.

➤ At 7:00 p.m., work out what type of commitment I am prepared to make to the company for the sponsorship. Write out a detailed proposal and have it ready one day prior to the meeting so I can run it by John and get his input.

➤ Call Rick, my investment advisor, today at 12:15 p.m. so we can set up a meeting to go over finances and calculate how much I must put away so I can go for the MBA and what my total commitment financially, considering worst case/no company help, will be to the MBA and what my financial options are.

➤ Join my career professional association today and submit a proposal for a paper by April 23rd. Send an e-mail to Brad to set up a meeting on Friday next week, early morning, to talk to Brad about attending the annual conference and to get company sponsorship.

➤ Ask Peter, the senior scientist, today to assist me with my paper and ask John at the meeting.

➤ On Saturday of this week at 11:00 a.m., update my resume and fix my profile on LinkedIn to reflect my management skills and my goal of becoming a director. Just in case things don't work out with Pfizer, I need a backup, and my profile needs to be seen. Begin developing my ProfessionaliBrand.

➤ Every week on Thursday before going home from work, spend a half hour building network by sending out LinkedIn invites, minimum of five, as well as contacting two prominent people in my field who are on professional committees, sending them my profile, and offering my help.

➤ Every three months, prepare a summary of accomplishments and targets, and during a meeting with John evaluate where I am and where I am going, and get help from John on redirecting or focusing as need be.

As you can see, these goals are SMART: Specific, Measurable, Action-oriented, Realistic/Relevant, and Time-specific.

EVA AND YOUR WISH LIST

Remember Eva? Go back and review my encounter with Eva. Use your dream actualization list and substitute at least one of your five-year dreams for mine. Follow Eva's instructions and write down your answers to all her questions.

"The Answer" Revealed

Now that you have followed Eva's instructions clearly you know what you want and how to start getting it. It is time to find out what Eva had written out on "The Answer." STOP. Only after you have completed your Eva encounter—I repeat: *only after*—otherwise, of course, your dream will not come true. If you have not done your Eva encounter, stop and go do it now.

What did Eva's "The Answer" reveal?

"The Answer": "If you listened to Eva's instructions carefully your wish has already started to actualize." Remember Eva's final instructions were, "When you have the first step clearly in your mind, open your eyes." So you now know your *first step*. Take it and everything will begin flowing from your first step. Remember "The Answer" and what it really means: **All you have to do is figure out your first step—and your dream will already start to actualize by taking the first step.**

DEFINING YOUR SMART GOALS

It's your turn to write SMART goals. Before you set out your goals and start acting on them, go for it but avoid taking on too much all at once. Most people fail to achieve their dreams because they try to change too much all at once. Make a committed decision to follow through at a pace you can handle and that will show consistent progress. It is best to start slow and achieve your dream than to burn out within one month of beginning. Remember: If you just improve by 1 percent per day, within 100 days you will have improved by 100 percent. Start at a sustainable pace. Remember your SCA. It is called a Sustainable Competitive Advantage for a specific reason: It must be sustainable!

It's your turn to write SMART goals for the following. Write out SMART goals for the achievement of your five-year dream.

- ➜ Write a clear description of your five-year dream.
- ➜ Write your first step—your answer to "The Answer."
- ➜ Write an action you can take today.
- ➜ Write your goals for the next five days.
- ➜ Write one weekly goal.
- ➜ Write one monthly goal.
- ➜ Write one six-month goal.
- ➜ Write one one-year goal.

➡ Write one two-year goal.

➡ Write one three-year goal.

Every day spend a half hour clearly writing out your goals or to-dos that you must accomplish the following day with respect to achieving your dream. Revisit your goals every six months and adjust forward accordingly. Set it in your calendar. As you work through the book the goals you must achieve with respect to getting the job you want will become very clear, and you can add to your list accordingly.

Remember: You know your first step, so take it now. Get started now and write your goals.

The next chapter will confirm that you have just aroused a particular part of your brain called the reticular activating system by setting goals. You have now programmed yourself, and subconsciously you will start gravitating toward achieving your goals.

CHAPTER 4

VISUALIZATION: THE PATH TO CONFIDENCE AND CERTAINTY

"When I was very young, I visualized myself being and having what it was I wanted. Mentally I never had any doubts about it. The mind is really so incredible. Before I won my first Mr. Universe, I walked around the tournament like I owned it. The title was already mine. I had won it so many times in my mind that there was no doubt I would win it. Then, when I moved on to the movies, the same thing. I visualized myself being a successful actor and earning big money. I could feel and taste success. I just knew it would all happen."

—Arnold Schwarzenegger[1]

What stops many of us from taking action? For most people, it is the lack of certainty. Without certainty we open the door to fear. When we are fearful we hesitate or we take no action at all. This is true when searching for a new job. As indicated previously, the loss of a job can lead to a loss of confidence.

The loss of confidence is a result of the uncertainty one feels about the when, what, where, and how of the next job. The same is true for transitioning to a better job. For some, the act of moving beyond one's comfort zone to reach for what they really want in a job can lead to the "Am I good enough?" uncertainty chorus usually followed by a cacophony of reasons and excuses to justify the not moving forward. The truth is, inadequacy and shame are the devils that taunt most job-seekers, be they employed and wanting a better new job, or be they unemployed and in need of a job. These devils are actually universal, even if most of us won't admit them. Those negative emotions control our actions more readily than we realize. They are energy-sapping emotions that are developed in childhood. The fact is that in both cases it is the unknown and the uncertainty of the unknown—the perceived expected outcome, that of rejection—reinforcing the feelings of inadequacy and shame for not being good enough, that have you backtracking and eventually settling for less. The facts are that you do not want to settle for less and you have by now clearly established that you want to reach your dreams. You need tools in addition to the brainwave technology you were introduced to earlier to get you to break through and manufacture the certainty you need to get the job you want. You will be called to take action as you progress through the book. Some of it may seem scary at first, and you will need to overcome the fear in order to move forward. Even if you think you are the most confident person in the world, at times everyone gets rattled, especially in job search, and you need techniques to get you back on track quickly.

HOPING VS. EXPECTING

Consider the difference between hoping to get a job and absolute expectation that you will get the job. Close your eyes and think about the job you hope you will get. How do you feel, and how does your body react to hoping to get the job you want? Think about what you would say—the exact words you would use when explaining to a friend that you hoped to get a job. Now open your eyes. Give it a minute. Now close your eyes and think about absolutely expecting to get the job. Take notice of the feelings you have as well as the signals your body is giving you. Think about what you would say—the words you would use when explaining to a friend that you absolutely expect to get the job. What is the difference between hoping and expecting? Most people in my seminars tell me the big difference is, when they are *hoping* they have a passive feeling and when they are *expecting* they feel as though they are active and taking action and they feel strong and certain about it happening. **In order to get what you want, you need to expect that you will get what you want.** If you expect this book will get you hired, it will—because you will have confidence as a result of feeling certain and therefore take the action necessary to make it happen. The transition from simply hoping to expecting is critical to getting what you want. This absolute expectancy is in fact the way to create certainty and remove fear.

How then do you create certainty in order to remove the fear that is blocking your progression? Yes, you may start out by hoping for something, but you must transition to absolute expectation or certainty in order to take the action that will get you the job you want or the job of your dreams.

Manufacturing Certainty Through Visualization

Unleashing your untapped potential can be realized by practicing focused visualization. I call this type of visualization "mindful visualization" because it requires awareness or consciousness of the act of visualization, and it requires using your mind to imagine the positive outcomes as real. It is not about short glimpses or seeing things, but rather more like watching a movie unfold. It is about being the integral part of the movie and actively participating in your visual process of achieving an outcome. It has a distinct purpose: to manufacture certainty and give you the impetus to take action. It is about being totally aware and focused on visualizing an event or process and the resultant positive outcome. It has been proven time after time that when people envision the result they want as actually having happened, or they create a series of vivid mental pictures of having reached their goals, they can achieve truly incredible results.

Here is an overview of the mindful visualization process. You vividly imagine the result you want (positive outcome) as already having been achieved. This creates *certainty*. This certainty gives you the confidence to *take action*. Taking action gives you *positive results*. The positive results then support the *positive beliefs* in yourself, which then *motivate* you to start over and take more action.

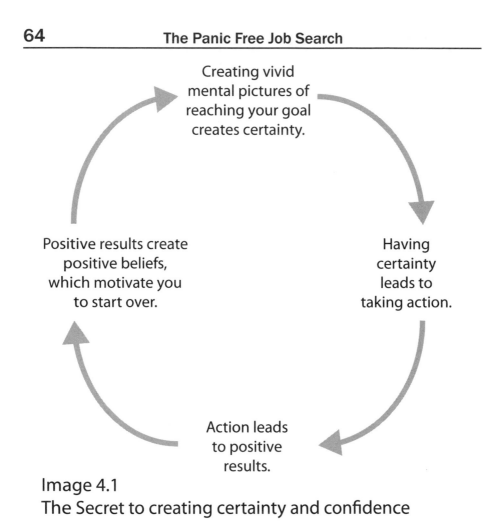

Creating vivid mental pictures of reaching your goal creates certainty.

Having certainty leads to taking action.

Action leads to positive results.

Positive results create positive beliefs, which motivate you to start over.

Image 4.1
The Secret to creating certainty and confidence

MINDFUL VISUALIZATION WORKS

Doing the Humanly Impossible

High-performance athletes use the process of mindful visualization as standard operating procedure. In the book *The Lore of Running*, Tim Noakes describes the story of Roger Bannister, the first person to run a mile in less than four minutes. At the time, it was believed to be humanly impossible. The technique that Roger Bannister used in preparing for this world-acclaimed record-shattering run was mindful visualization. How did he apply this technique to achieve his goal of breaking the four-minute mile? Roger would run the race over and over in his mind, each time visualizing breaking the four-minute barrier. He pictured exactly how he entered the corners, when he would accelerate, and when he would vary his pace. In fact, he had broken the four-minute barrier hundreds of times in his mind by the time he attempted it on that famous day. When race day came, he had *certainty* and he knew he would attain his dream. He broke the four-minute mile—that is, he ran the mile in less than four minutes. (Go to *www.transitiontohired.com/resources* to watch a video of the race.)

Do we all have the same potential to be successful? I believe we do, as Roger Bannister and countless others have proven.

See it in the mind's eye, see it unfold, and you can make it happen.

Is it possible to gain muscle strength without exercising and by just using your mind? In a scientific paper, "From Mental Power to Muscle Power—Gaining Strength by Using the Mind," the researchers clearly showed you can![2] The purpose of the study was to determine if strength gain could be induced using only the mind or mental training (without performing physical exercises) in the little finger abductor as well as in the elbow flexor muscles. In a study consisting of three groups, the ABD group did mental training concentrating on increasing strength in the little finger, the ELB group did mental training concentrating on increasing elbow muscle strength, and of course there was a control group, which participated in all measurements but no mental training.

Draw your own conclusion about how outstanding the results of mental training for strength gain are. The ABD group saw an increase of 35 percent in strength. That is correct: 35 percent! The ELB group saw an increase of 13.5 percent and the control group saw no significant difference. The conclusion is that you can gain muscle strength without traditional exercise by simply muscle training with your mind.

Still a non-believer? Check out the alternate study discussed in the article "Strength Gains by Motor Imagery with Different Ratios of Physical to Mental Practice." The study subjects performed strength training exercises over a set schedule. The study "concluded that high-intensity strength training sessions can be partly replaced by IMC training sessions without any considerable reduction of strength gains."[3] (IMC stands for "imagined maximal isometric contraction," which means simply imagining your muscles contracting.)

Your mind is powerful beyond belief, and the best news is *you are in charge of it*, which makes you powerful beyond belief.

Test the Power of Mindful Visualization Yourself

Okay, you still don't believe me. Stand up. Put your arms straight out, parallel with the ground, and with your index fingers pointing straight out also. Keep your feet planted and facing forward. See how far you can twist your arms around your torso by turning to the right without moving your feet. Come on, as far as you can go. Now come back to a resting position. Close your eyes and extend your arms and fingers the same way. Visualize your arm going 25 percent farther—really feel it. Now visualize it going 50 percent farther—really see it. Now visualize it 75 percent farther, now 100 percent. Open your eyes, and with your feet firmly planted, instead of simply visualizing it, actually do it. How far did you go? I bet at least 25-percent farther, correct? Amazing! Yes, you have more potential than you think.

All you need to do is visualize your success and take the necessary action, and you will get what you visualize!

GREATNESS THROUGH IMAGINATION AND VISUALIZATION

Throughout history great performers and thinkers attribute achievement to a great imagination or the act of visualization. The greatest recipe for success I have found and that I use is eloquently described by author Alfred A. Montapert, who said "To accomplish great things we must first dream, then visualize, then plan...believe...act!"[4] Visualization is not a new concept; it has been described going back more than a century as a "law of psychology." William James (1842–1910), psychologist and author, stated, "There is a law in psychology that if you form a picture in your mind of what you would like to be, and you keep and hold that picture there long enough, you will soon become exactly as you have been thinking."[5]

Many who came after William James came to the same conclusion—that visualization leads to improving performance. One thing is very clear: You can be certain that using visualization to increase performance has been proven to work for many beyond the world of sport, including one of the greatest minds ever. Albert Einstein said, "Imagination is more important than knowledge."[6] I don't know about you, but I believe throwing my hat in the ring with Albert is a very safe bet.

The Brain Science of Visualization

Common to athletes, musicians, and other performers is the use of visualization as a form of "mental rehearsal." Research shows that "practicing in your mind" is almost as effective as practicing physically, and doing both is more effective than either one alone.

Tom Venuto makes the case for the scientific validation of the power of visualizations in an excellent article in which he quotes Dr. Richard Restak, a neuroscientist and author of books about the human brain:

> The process of imagining yourself going through the motions of a complex musical or athletic performance activates brain areas that improve your performance. Brain scans have placed such intuitions on a firm neurological basis. Positron emission tomography (PET) scans reveal that the mental rehearsal of an action activates the prefrontal areas of the brain responsible for the formulation of the appropriate motor programs. In practical terms, this means you can benefit from the use of mental imagery.[7]

Can you see the benefit of using mindful visualization to help you perform at a peak level through the stressful situations that are presented throughout the process of a job search?

Overcoming Cancer by Visualization

How powerful is visualization? Is it possible to use mindful visualization to communicate with and control your body's cells, organs, and tissues?

Dr. Carl Simonton, a physician and cancer researcher, treated his patients with radiation and also taught them how to visualize their immune cells "munching away" at cancer cells. Simonton and his wife, psychologist Stephanie Matthews-Simonton, disclosed the results of their work with cancer patients, which indicated a link between visualization and treating cancer, in the 1970s. According to Carol Greenhouse, writing in *Ode Magazine,* "Of 159 patients, whose average life expectancy was 12 months, 63 lived at least two years, and 19 percent of those were cancer-free after a combination of radiation and Simonton's imagery techniques. The tumors shrank in another 22 percent after the same treatment."[8]

YOUR GOALS ON AUTO-PILOT

For those who thought visualization was for nuts and crazies, or just for athletes, it is time to rethink. Or if you think you have a great excuse now for not achieving because you claim you can't visualize well, you will have to find a new excuse. The human brain and your subconscious are incredible creations of nature. What if you could attract what you want by setting a goal, mapping out your strategy, and letting your subconscious take over? It has been demonstrated that your subconscious will filter out the erroneous inputs and focus you on the things that draw you closer to your goal.

Neuroscientist Nancy Andreasen writes, "Our ability to filter unnecessary stimuli and focus our attention is mediated by brain mechanisms in the thalamus and the reticular activating system."[9] The reticular activating system (RAS) is important because it acts to alert you to the things that are important so you will take notice.

Have you ever bought a shirt and then gone out in public and noticed how many people have the same shirt? The reason you notice so many shirts is because your RAS has been aroused. "The RAS consists of a bundle of densely packed nerve cells located in the central core of the brainstem. Roughly the size of a little finger, the RAS runs from the top of the spinal cord into the middle of the brain. This area of tightly packed nerve fibers and cells contain nearly 70% of your brain's estimated 200 billion nerve cells or about 140 billion cells."[10]

The RAS, in combination with your thalamus, can act to select, filter, and give you focus. All you have to do is have a clear and specific goal, and let your RAS take over. When you have a clear goal, your RAS pays attention to the goal and finds ways to achieve it. As long as you focus on your goal your RAS screens out all the erroneous stuff. All you have to do is take the appropriate action.

In other words, your subconscious being deductive will guide you to achieving your goal by focusing your behavior, attitude, and attention; all you have to do is perform the actual action that is necessary.

MANUFACTURING CERTAINTY IN AN INSTANT

Now you can see the true power of understanding wishes, dreams, and goals and how you can make your dreams come true. The science is there to back it up. Set your goals, visualize, and overcome your fears by creating certainty so you can take action and get what you want. You can be confident that your body and brain have the mechanisms to get you what you want if you clearly pick out a goal.

I believe science someday will provide us with conclusive proof that visualization actually does cause cellular, and therefore physiological, changes in the body and in fact is much more powerful than we ever imagined.

Would knowing how to create certainty or being able to call up unwavering confidence be a great tool to have? In order to achieve the ultimate level of success, you need to first create certainty in order to have the confidence to take the first step and follow through with the tough actions that are often necessary to achieve the results you want. You can create certainty by learning a very simple technique I call "getting in state." You have seen fighters or athletes get super-focused before an event, and in many cases you may have noticed certain actions they perform (pumping a fist, or banging their head on a turnbuckle, or slapping themselves). What are they actually doing? They are getting into state—the state of absolute certainty—before their event. I used the technique I am about to reveal often—and used it many times throughout the three years it took me to write this book. Becoming a published author can be a lonely, trying endeavor fraught with much rejection and criticism along the way to success. You can use this same technique to help you get in peak state and overcome reluctance to take action when you have to tackle something you consider difficult, or even after a setback to get you back on track and confident.

Creating Your Anchor

Close your eyes and visualize a time in the past when you were really on top of your game—when you felt unstoppable and incredible. Take the time to really let that feeling and vision sink in. When you are in this peak state and you can really feel that feeling of being on top of the world, create an anchor. You create an anchor by making a physical move (your move) as well as screaming out a word that feels powerful for you. My trademark move is three reverse fist pumps, by forming a fist, and bending my arm and pulling it into my body while I scream out "Yes" three times in unison with my fist-pumping action. Now create your move. As you are in that peak state, make sure to make your move with more and more speed and exuberance, and scream out very loudly.

How can you use this in job search? Prior to starting out on your job search plan for the day, every morning get in state. Launch your anchor; make your move over and over until you are really pumped. In the peak state you just created, begin your visualization. The key is to use as many imaginary senses as you can; see, feel, touch, and smell the things that are associated with the ideal job or target for you.

For instance, if the target is a job working with horses, visualize a stable; smell the hay and the horse manure, and really get into it.

Perhaps it is in an office position. See yourself at your desk; see the coffee machine, the male or female assistant, and everything you possibly can in the surroundings. Get extremely detailed. See yourself cashing that first paycheck for more money than you have ever made. See the actual amount and name of the company on the check. See yourself on vacation with more vacation time than you had previously. Really work hard on these visualizations; make it real. Then launch your anchor again. Make your move many times—get really pumped up. Follow through with your action items on your daily plan. Use this technique throughout the day as needed to keep yourself pumped up and to visualize positive outcomes.

For example, when you are about to make a networking call:

➤ Start by visualizing a positive call with a positive end result (for instance, the person helping you out or saying yes to a meeting).

➤ Get into a peak state by releasing your anchor—that is, make your move.

➤ Stand up while making your call and put a smile on your face.

Now you are in a state of certainty and you will get more positive results. I guarantee it.

Use the process of mindful visualization over and over again. Through repetition you will be able to create positive beliefs to keep you moving toward achieving your goals on the way to achieving your dream(s). Put it into practice and you will get the job you want.

Put into practice: Certainty = Actions = Results = Positive Beliefs.

See and focus on a positive end result, take action, and you will get positive results, and this will lead to strengthening a system of positive beliefs. If you get negative results (and you will at times), go back to getting absolutely certain, use your anchor, and start the process again. Positive results will happen.

Let the positive results feed your positive beliefs and you will get what you focus on.

PART III

TACTICS

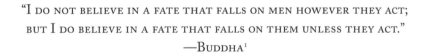

CHAPTER 5

SMART SEARCH

> "I DO NOT BELIEVE IN A FATE THAT FALLS ON MEN HOWEVER THEY ACT;
> BUT I DO BELIEVE IN A FATE THAT FALLS ON THEM UNLESS THEY ACT."
> —BUDDHA[1]

INTRODUCTION TO SMART SEARCH AND BUILDING A TARGET LIST

Whether you had lost the will to take action, or you were dissatisfied with your job search and career progress, this system works through alignment, confidence, and taking tactical action. By this point in your journey, you have clearly determined your competence, your passion, and your Sustainable Competitive Advantage (SCA). You've built your confidence, adjusted your self-talk to be empowering, and you have the gift of using visualization to move you forward and achieve your career dream. You now know what leads to achieving fulfillment and what the key principles of career satisfaction are. You also know the detrimental health consequences of not taking action.

Hopefully you are ready to take action to find a job meeting your criteria by deploying the innovative and proven tactics you are about to learn. Once you have defined the parameters of your job search, from where you want to live and work to the type and size of company, built the resume and profile that will attract attention, and created a strong ProfessionaliBrand, you will be fully prepared to reap the rewards of Smart Search.

In order to make the choices that are right for you, you have to understand the shortcomings of conventional search techniques, from answering ads by e-mailing your resume or responding through an employer's Website, to using the services of a search firm or an employment agency.

Only 9 percent of professional and technical positions are filled by search firms, according to Harvard sociologist Mark S. Granovetter.[2] The same analysis finds that only 10 percent of such jobs are filled by advertising, wheras informal contacts, such as networking and marketing to contacts, account for nearly 80 percent of job placements. This study is supported by more recent studies. According to a study reported on Forbes.com by webjob.com, 23 percent of recent job-seekers got their jobs through advertisements.[3] In a related article on Forbes.com, Susan Adams restates webjob.com's findings and claims that the remaining 77 percent (or three out of four, as she puts it) got their jobs through people they know, what we call networking and referrals, and by targeting and contacting employers directly or by mass mailing to employers regardless of whether they had jobs advertised.[4]

In the best-case scenario, new jobs are found by "clicking and sending" only in about 25 percent of situations.

Job boards have low success rates, and the best research available shows that the success rate of famous job boards such as Monster.com, HotJobs.com, and CareerBuilder.com is still dubious at best. The job boards tend to be over-populated and bear little fruit for the job-seeker. The "reply to the advertisement" approach on job boards is dead as an effective vehicle to getting the job you want. This was confirmed, as far back as 2002, by Mark Mehler and Gerry Crispin, principals of MMC Group, in reporting the results of their study that only 3.6 percent of all external hires at the companies in their study were attributed to Monster.com.[5]

More notably, something big happened in the online job market in October 2010 that makes the use of job boards even more questionable: "Job search engine Indeed.com slipped past Monster.com to become the largest job site in the U.S. according to comScore."[6]

Why is this so significant? The growth of Indeed once again suggests the power of search can trump everything else and how important search engine search is to job search.

JOB SEARCH IN THE NEW JOB-SEARCH REALITY IS ABOUT BEING FOUND

When you understand the power of Internet search, and the power of the Web 3.0 (the trail of your private or public information, that is being tracked) you understand the power of being found by employers, recruiters, and decision-makers. You also understand the importance of your profile being represented by the right keywords, and furthermore you have a good understanding of the relationship of keywords to job search, as well as their corresponding relationship to online search. By exploiting keywords and Search Engine Optimization (SEO) to your advantage, you have the ability today of dominating the top spots of employers' and recruiters' search engine and LinkedIn search results. The idea is to show up in the top results of their searches. This way you can become the candidate they pursue and hire. This requires building a ProfessionaliBrand that gets you to the top of search results for the likes of Google, Yahoo, and Bing. Coupling this with an effective professional social media strategy is the key to being irresistible to employers and recruiters and being offered jobs.

ProfessionaliBranding is about promoting and managing the online message about you as a professional. A compelling ProfessionaliBrand leads to attracting employers and recruiters so you'll never, ever have to look for another job again. Smart Search is all about being a candidate without having to be an applicant first! (Much more on how to be a candidate through ProfessionaliBranding in Chapter 7.)

With this knowledge, you need to divide your time and energy relative to where your job search success is likely going to come from, and that is developing informal contacts through online networking (LinkedIn, Facebook, Google+, and Twitter), through direct marketing, and through traditional networking. Effective job-search networking today is a blend of online and offline tactics: making contact online and taking the relationship offline through a telephone, video, or face-to-face meeting. In other words, job search today is no longer about searching for jobs, or job postings on the Internet, rather it is about people search—finding the right people through search and networking that will lead you to your next job, or attracting the right professionals to you through a powerful online presence that results in getting hired.

AGGRESSIVE JOB SEARCH IS ABOUT TARGETED MARKETING

If you are unemployed and late to the party, and have not developed an effective ProfessionaliBrand or even at the minimum a great LinkedIn profile that consistently shows up in employers' and recruiters' searches, you may find yourself in need of an aggressive approach to getting hired. This is where direct marketing is effective: you are the hunter and you hunt down other professionals and decision-makers in order to find work. If you are unemployed, of course using a combination of Smart Search methods, including ProfessionaliBranding, direct marketing, and networking, among others, will get you hired faster.

LET GO OF YOUR OLD PROGRAMMING

If the vast majority of professional and technical job placements take place through networking and informal contacts, are advertisements, job boards, and recruiters (headhunters) deserving of a great deal of your time? You decide! Most job-seekers will focus 100 percent of their time on something that at best may have a 10- to 25-percent success rate: "clicking and sending" their resume to job postings and directly to targets without a strategy.

Why do people do this? Because it is easy and comfortable! This form of search does not require truly investing "you," your reputation, and passion. This way the "you" is protected against feeling rejection, a very uncomfortable feeling for many. If you keep burying your head in the sand, and using "click and send" by responding to postings/job advertisements on the Internet, then you deserve what you get.

Focus on what gets results: Smart Search!

GET INSIDE THE MINDS OF THE DECISION-MAKERS

Okay, so where do you go to get a great job? You go where the jobs are—behind the corporate gates and inside the minds of the decision-makers and hiring managers. I'll show you how to get there.

Smart Search tactics focus your efforts on the strategies that the research we've mentioned previously says accounts for 75 out of 100 new hires. There are three key components to Smart Search:

Attracting and Promoting

➜ ProfessionaliBranding—developing an irresistible Internet presence

➜ Creating a positive reputation through social media and cleaning up your Internet footprint

Networking

➜ Social networking sites (LinkedIn, Facebook, Twitter, Google+, and so forth)

➜ Job Search Talking

Direct Marketing

➜ Targeting, presentation marketing, engagement marketing, fear-based marketing

The components of Smart Search are complementary and do depend to a great extent today on having a compelling ProfessionaliBrand. Even though you may still be hellbent on playing the "click and send" lottery, hoping to tap into that 25-percent success rate, you need a compelling ProfessionaliBrand. According to an article by Kashmir Hill, a survey done by Reppler (a social media monitoring service designed to help users manage their online image) found that 91 percent of the 300 "hiring types" (employers) surveyed are doing social media screens of applicants.[7] It is also noteworthy to find out from this same reporter that "Almost half of them started Googling right after receiving an application. The rest of them waited until the hiring process was further along."[8] Of this same group, 69 percent indicated they had rejected someone based on what they found on the Internet. The article also provides insight into this question: Can (and does) a social networking profile and a web presence help you get hired? It is quite clear from the following that it does. "Before you go ahead and delete or deactivate your Facebook account, note that Reppler also asked the job granters the converse: how often social networking profiles contributed to a candidate getting hired. Heartening news: That turned out to be the case for 68% of them."[9] It is clear even if you want to stick to the old-school applying to jobs through job boards or adverts you need a powerful ProfessionaliBrand to sway your potential future employers because 91 percent are checking you out online. The bottom line is this: Regardless of the approach you take to job search today, you need a powerful ProfessionaliBrand to get hired, not a devaluing personal brand that might be hurting you (or none at all, which is telling in itself by its absence, considering that most employers today seek some advanced technology proficiency in their new employees).

Putting Smart Search Into Action

We've now reached the point in the book where the rubber hits the road (or the hockey stick hits the ice, if you are Canadian). The Smart Search approach is about becoming visible and findable through ProfessionaliBranding, researching and targeting employers, using your network to generate more referrals than you thought possible, and direct marketing. The Smart Search method boils down to getting off your you-know-what and tapping your inner Rambo: You take control of your outcomes. You do not sit back and wait; you plan and take action.

The Smart Search strategy is explained in this chapter followed with in-depth guidance on the benefits and execution of Smart Search in the following chapters. In order to execute the Smart Search strategy you need to first understand what it is as well as define your job-search parameters.

The Smart Search Strategy

➤ Define your job-search parameters.

➤ Build a resume targeted to your employer list.

➤ Build your full ProfessionaliBrand (at a minimum your LinkedIn profile).

➤ Target decision-makers through networking and/or direct marketing.

➤ Understand the advantages and disadvantages of using headhunters. (Go to *www.transitiontohired.com/resources* for in-depth information on this topic).

Defining Your Smart Search Parameters

The first objective is to find employers, do research on the employers, and then select them based on your criteria in order to make a target list. This list and the research you do will be indispensable to any and all Smart Search methods you decide to use. Defining your parameters involves clearly defining:

➤ **Geography:** where you want to live and work

➤ **Size:** small, medium, or large employer

➤ **Type:** public or private corporation, public or private institution, or small business, like a sole proprietorship

➤ **Position:** job title and/or level

➤ **Position Category:** universal or specialist

⇨ *Universal:* this job category is one that is found in most companies (for example, accounting or sales-related positions)

⇨ *Specialist:* very specialized skill set; fewer employers to choose from (for example, nuclear scientist). Mobility and flexibility in geography are bonuses for the job-seeker

Geography
Where are you prepared to live and work?
www.city-data.com

Job Category
Specialist or universal?
www.bls.gov/soc/

Type of Employer
Private, public, small, large, culture?
www.manta.com/coms2/page_worldwide

Image 5.1
Define your job search parameters

A great resource to download and have on your browser is a free toolbar that will give you access to company information and directories at your finger tips. Go to *www.transitiontohired.com/resources.*

To Avoid Overwhelm, "Chunk"

It is highly recommended that you use a "chunk" strategy as an effective way of organizing your search. Figuratively speaking, to chunk means to break things down in small, bite-size pieces, and then consume one bite at a time. Why is it important to chunk?

It has been my experience that people get caught up in the research. They create great beautiful lists of 300 company names. Once they have exhausted themselves creating the list, they sit back, look at the list, and become overwhelmed. The thought of targeting 300 employers scares the crap out of them and they never take action. Compiling such a big list can take a week or more. During that time there is no positive feedback coming in for their efforts, creating a feedback loop that results in feelings of despair. Limit your list to 40 targeted potential employers. This size list is manageable.

Once you have exhausted your first list then go on and create an additional list. Rarely have any of my clients had to go higher than a 40-employer list in any industry when using the Smart Search system.

Geography

Evaluate where you want to work, and the type of city you want to work in. Consider your family needs and your interests when doing your research.

For a site that is simply incredible, has a wealth of information, and is all free—and we like free—see Image 5.1 for the link to city data. Relevant information includes real estate, population male-to-female ratios, income levels, crime stats, schools, average temperature, sunshine days, even average wind speed. You name it, it has it. It also has pictures of specific sites throughout the city of interest so you can get a feel for the area.

ESTABLISHING POSITION CATEGORY

The position category you are seeking, be it universal or specialized, will determine which companies you should focus on. Information is also available on occupations, universal or specialist; see the link in Image 5.1.

Universal Position Category

If you have a universal position, such as an accounting-related position, most medium-sized or large employers will have these types of positions. Your choice of companies is usually enormous. This is where your must make sure to chunk your research and start working your list once you have reached 30 or 40 employer targets.

Specialist Position Category

If you are a rocket scientist, or want a specialist position, your choices are more limited and require a niche search.

This is where you must become creative.

Want to increase your options? If your background and skills put you into the specialized category, review your skills from a functional (see Chapter 6) and transferable, rather than a specialized, perspective.

When is this useful? This is useful when you are limited and/or have no choices for work in your preferred geographical location. If your functional skills make it possible, shift your search to a universal position category.

It can also be useful if you have a passion for a specialized type of work, but you have no experience in that area. You might need to first break into the industry or company and pay your dues, by taking an ad hoc position in order to get the exposure you need, with the goal of eventually getting hired into the specialist position you are really passionate about. In other words, you are paying your dues in order to get what you really want.

In most cases your skills will be transferable across industries.

CHOOSING COMPANY TYPE AND SIZE

Determine what type of company you want to work for. For example, do you want to work for a sole proprietorship, a small or private company, a large publicly traded company, an educational institution, or a non-profit organization? Please note: Do not overlook small companies and sole proprietorships; the real "job nectar" is often with small companies.

According to an Intuit Future of Small Business Report, "Large-company employment has fallen steadily for several decades. Today, less than 40% of Americans work for companies with more than 1,000 employees. At the same time, small business employment continues to climb in absolute numbers, and as a percentage of total employment."[10]

My view is that if corporations could have feelings, then large corporations have no feelings. Their Websites will tell you all the warm and fuzzy stuff about how they value their employees. I find that small businesses, on the other hand, have feelings. Often owners of small businesses will go without paying themselves to keep their employees. I have rarely heard of this kind of sacrifice from the "big ones." The reality in the world of corporate downsizing, firing, layoffs, and/or right-sizing is that the process is simply brutal and callous, as this quotaton from MSNBC.com clearly demonstrates:

"They gave me no help. Nothing. Just 'Have a nice day'," said Joanne, 51, who asked that we use only her first name. "It was a horrible way to treat people. It was unbelievable."[11]

USING DIRECTORIES AND SEARCH ENGINES TO GENERATE EMPLOYER LISTS

You can use industry-specific directories, professional association directories, and specialty search engines to find employers. You can get a list of these resources at *www.transitiontohired.com/resources,* as well as a list of job search portals and a list of portals and services that offer employer ratings (in other words, the "dirt" or "intel" on what it is like working at a specific employer).

Expanding Your Search

Unfortunately, finding a "one-stop shop" directory and/or specialty search engine that will give you everything you seek with respect to a comprehensive company list is usually a lost cause. Usually, you need to use a few different directories and search engines and/or strategies.

In order to augment your research and find those elusive companies, you may want to use the likes of search engines such as Google, Yahoo, or Bing, especially if you are seeking a specialist position. In order to save time as well as find what you are looking for you need to know how to perform specific LinkedIn or Google searches, or even Google searches of the LinkedIn site. The use of LinkedIn is preferred to generate a list of companies because you can migrate quickly to search for contact names within the site or use Google again to search for contact names within LinkedIn.

Using Google's Search Power to Search LinkedIn's Site

Beyond the specialized directories, I prefer to use Google to scour the business networking site LinkedIn, in order to generate a list of companies. What does scouring LinkedIn mean? It means using Google's power to do a search of the LinkedIn database. The tricks you will find in this chapter are invaluable. Beyond getting the names of the employers, these best practices will allow you to circumvent the need to have an extensive network of connections on LinkedIn when you are at the point of seeking contacts, at the employers of choice, to use in your Smart Search implementation. Typically speaking, in order to access the full LinkedIn database you need to have a premium account. If you do not have a premium account, your searches are limited to 100 results. If you use Google to X-ray the LinkedIn site, you do not need these connections or the costly premium feature.

VERY IMPORTANT:

If you only get a few search results in Google from using the following strings, make sure to click on *"repeat the search with the omitted results."*

Also make sure to respect the integrity of the string; spaces and quotes signs must be adhered to.

Note that for every specific search described you will be pointed to a table that provides the exact search string. Simply copy as given, enter into the Google search bar, and customize a few words relevant to your specific job-search parameters in order to generate the search results you require for your employer list.

Table 5.1 Plug and Search – Google Search Strings

Search	Keyword	String	Example
Search 1	Google/LinkedIn companies search—"universal position"	inurl:LinkedIn.com/companies "City"	inurl:LinkedIn.com/companies "Boston"
Search 2	Google/LinkedIn companies search—"specialist position"	inurl:LinkedIn.com/companies intitle:LinkedIn Industry companies intitle: "job speciality" or a "title" "city"	inurl:LinkedIn.com/companies intitle: LinkedIn Pharmaceutical "Scientist" "Greater Boston area"
Search 3	Google Search String small employers (for example, for Toronto)	"Testimonials" "area code" or "zip"	"Testimonials" "416 OR 905 OR 647"
Search 4	Large publicly traded companies in your geographical preference area (for example, for San Francisco)	-jobs "careers" "area or zip code" "investor relations" "annual meeting"	-jobs "careers" "415" "investor relations" "annual meeting"
Search 5	Publicly traded company located in Detroit	-jobs "careers" "area or zip code" "investor relations" "annual meeting" "key word(s)"	-jobs "careers" "313" "investor relations" "annual meeting" "automotive parts"

To get the search strings in a ready-to-go format, simply go to *www.transitiontohired.com* and copy the search strings and paste into Google.

GetHiredFastTrack "plug and play" search strings for LinkedIn Companies:

- To find employers for universal positions: See Search 1 in Table 5.1.
- To find employers for specialist positions: See Search 2 in Table 5.1.

Using Google to Search by Company Structure or Size

Going through directories can be very time consuming with respect to determining the size or legal structure of a company, as well as the company's location. Many directories do not provide an option to search by size, private or public, or even location, and that leaves a lot of leg work. How to get around these limitations in order for you to get a quick start? The following search strings will provide results based on size and type of company.

Searching for Small Employers Using Google

Use the word *testimonials* in your search criteria, because most small companies, as opposed to large companies, will have a "testimonials" page for credibility purposes on their Website. Use telephone area codes to define geography. As an example, to find small enterprises in Toronto, Ontario, Canada, use the three area codes that are representative of the region. The Toronto area and city has three area codes, so you would search: 416 or 905 or 647.

- Google search string for small employers: See Search 3 in Table 5.1.

Searching for Large Publicly Traded Companies Using Google

Large companies will usually have a "careers" section on their Website. Because we want publicly traded corporations, it stands to reason that the Websites will have an "investor relations" section and the words *annual meeting*. For example, if you wanted to search for publicly traded companies located in the San Francisco area, use the area code 415. Use the minus symbol and the word jobs (-jobs), which in search language means "no search results containing the word *jobs*." Why? Because most "job sites", such as Monster, CareerBuilder, and so forth use the word *jobs* in their Websites; large publicly traded companies rarely use that word on their site. As clearly stated previously, you want to stay away from job sites in today's job-search world. They are not as effective as they used to be in getting you hired.

- Google search string for large publicly traded companies: See Search 4 in Table 5.1

Google Search Strings for Specialist Positions

For identifying companies relevant to specialist positions, use the same criteria to differentiate small companies versus publicly traded corporations within a specific location or geography and add a specialty keyword(s) to the search string.

- Google search string for large publicly traded company located in Detroit specializing in automotive parts: See Search 5 in Table 5.1.

Once you get the hang of it you can create your own search strings.

> Google Search Tips: To indicate that search results must contain this word or this phrase, use the word(s) in quotes (" "). Use the minus sign (-) to indicate must *not* contain this word. For example: "Detroit" "Lansing," or for a phrase, "Detroit Michigan." You can also substitute a postal code or zip number for the telephone area codes. Make sure there is no space between the quotes (" ") and the adjoining word or the minus sign (-) and the adjoining word.
>
> Use OR to signify search results must contain either of the words, or in this case area codes in the search results. OR must be capitalized, and note the correct spacing: one space before and after OR.
>
> You can use AND in the same fashion. As an example, "416 AND 905 AND 647" means the results must contain all area codes.

Once you have done your research and selected your target employers and created your comprehensive list, the next step in your Smart Search strategy is to create a customizable resume.

CHAPTER 6

BUILD THE RESUME THAT GETS PICKED

"IF YOU CALL FAILURES EXPERIMENTS, YOU CAN PUT THEM IN YOUR RESUME AND CLAIM THEM AS ACHIEVEMENTS."

—MASON COOLEY[1]

It is an evil that must be mastered, because at some point in the "job-getting process" you will need to produce one. Yes, folks—the dreaded resume. Because a resume is necessary—particularly so for job-seekers who exclusively rely on a "click and send" approach to job search—you must develop the most effective, achievement-oriented, keyword-rich, competency-based resume in order to be picked by the applicant tracking systems (ATSs) and humans that guard the corporate inner sanctum. The resume also acts as the building block for the development of your online profiles, such as LinkedIn, and your online resume (iResumePro), which will soon usurp the traditional resume.

For "click and senders," the resume is your only true weapon to getting noticed. For others the resume is simply a tool in an effective job-search strategy, and they realize that it is not the resume but what you do with the resume that determines a successful job search, as well as how well your resume is supported by a strong Internet professional image. Make no mistake: Employers are Googling you and spying on you through the Web 3.0 (the technology that enables the ability to identify *"you"* and track the trail of your public or private information, as well as the use of this data).

In a tight economy with a high unemployment rate, you need to be prepared for a job war, and you need to apply yourself to crafting a customizable resume with all the key best practices elements regardless of the job strategy you deploy. Many resumes that I review do the candidate a disservice, and I want to make sure your resume does not get you kicked off the planet.

Why did I say dreaded? The reason is that resumes are ever evolving in the "human resources make it as complicated as possible" field. There are many theories and just as many books on resume writing, so what are you supposed to do? What type of resume should you write? What I want to do is to simplify this topic and present you with a resume-writing "how to" that will be state-of-the-art—but still simple enough for you to understand. This book is not a book on resume writing; it is a book that will provide you with effective and proven resume-writing instructions, and will, coupled with the job-search strategies extolled, get you hired. If you want more information or want to study resume writing there are many books dedicated to resume writing, including *Competency-Based Resumes: How to Bring Your Resume to the Top of the Pile* by Robin Kessler and Linda A. Strasburg (Career Press, 2005).

If your old resume type is no longer working for you and no longer getting you interviews, then it is time to pay attention and make some changes, including reviewing your Internet footprint, which may be hurting you. There is much confusion surrounding what should be on a resume. In order to create an effective resume that gets picked, you need answers to the following:

➤ What questions does the resume need to answer?

➤ What type of resume should you use?

➤ What style and format is appropriate?

➤ What is a competency-based resume?

➤ Why are keywords important?

➤ How are accomplishments and competencies tied together?

➜ How do you grab the reader's attention?

➜ Is your resume consistent, and does it "sync up" with your online footprint or profiles?

ONE SIZE FITS ALL, OR A CUSTOMIZED RESUME?

There are two approaches to the resume: have one resume and use it for all jobs and write a cover letter specific to the job you are applying for, or tailor your resume specifically for each new employer or decision-maker you connect with. Each approach of course has its merits but most professionals who are time-strapped want a one-size-fits-all resume. They want things simple; they do not believe in writing—or are unwilling to write—a resume for each job they apply for, even though our data clearly shows this is the best approach.

The typical approach to writing a resume is to outline your skills, background, and accomplishments, and hope that these match up with what the employer is looking for. The new thinking, and the one I advocate, is the competency-based approach. Using this approach you evaluate the employer's or the decision-maker's needs first (you do the research) and then the resume is written to demonstrate how your competencies match up with the job-specific needs and the organization's needs. Wait! Before you throw away the book, I promise to make the concept of competencies easier to understand and remove the confusion around the subject.

Of course the second approach—customizing your resume for every position you apply to—is the ideal approach, and this is where all the research you just did in compiling your employer target list can be used to customize your resume to address the needs of each individual employer. The GetHired-FastTrack competency-based resume is based on this premise of a customized resume for each employer and resume submission. Following this approach increases the likelihood that your resume will get picked.

As indicated previously, for many professionals this is not practical, or they just do not want to put the effort into it. Most professionals today want a resume that can be used over and over again, and that is state-of the-art and leading-edge in its representation of current organizational theory and practice. If you group yourself in the mainstream, then say hello to the competency-based resume. For many who want to write a competency-based resume, the stumbling block surrounds understanding what an actual competency is and which competencies are important to include in the resume.

THE IMPORTANCE OF UNDERSTANDING THE COMPETENCY-BASED SYSTEM

Having a passion and getting hired in a job you are passionate about are very distinct things. You must be able to express your passion for a particular job or occupation to an employer in the employer's language. You must be able to demonstrate your passion as well as your competence—that is, your potential ability to do the job you want. In other words, you must demonstrate you have the skills, knowledge, and style required to do the job at an acceptable level.

Your fit for a job is no longer measured by your strengths and weaknesses, but rather how your skills, knowledge, style, and behavior match up with the performance standards established for the position you want.

In human resources circles today, the determination of your compatibility for a job centers around determining your actual past performance based on performance indicators called competencies. Although many evangelists would like to convince you that competency-based HR management systems take the guesswork out of hiring and are scientifically based, my experience has been that making this system, or any other hiring or performance evaluation system, work is still a mixture of art and science.

The following statement or a variant of it shows up in most papers written on the subject: "The concept of competence has different meanings and it remains one of the most diffuse terms in the management development sector, and the organizational and occupational litterature."[2]

The bottom line is there is still much confusion about the words *competence, competency,* and *competencies* in the literature as well as with the HR professionals polled on the subject for this book.

If it is such a confusing area why am I addressing it in the book?

You cannot look anywhere in the job search or HR world without seeing competency this or competency that. The hiring game today is about competency-based systems, competence, competency-based resumes, competency-based interviews, competency profiles, and competencies as performance standards.

If you do not understand the game how can you play it?

If the referees—the decisions-makers that make the hiring decisions—don't understand the game, how can they select you? You need to understand the game in order to be able to play the game as well as educate and guide the decision-makers during their evaluations. According to Robin Kessler and Linda A. Strasburg, in their excellent book *Competency-Based Resumes*, "Understanding the system when looking for a job has always given certain candidates the advantage with employers. But it is critical to realize and accept that the system that employers use when making the decision to fill jobs has changed significantly in the last few years and continues to change today."[3] If you know more about the system than the line manager who is interviewing you, often you can make yourself shine by making his job easier and answering questions in a way that makes it simple for him to enter your answers into HR's evaluation system, and thereby sparing him a severe brain cramp. Why do I say a severe brain cramp? Because often the "HR Einsteins Gone Wild" force their line managers to evaluate competencies like "strategic agility"!

Regardless of whether you agree or disagree with the competency-based selection process, the fact is that many Fortune 500 companies and smaller employers are using competency-based systems. You need to understand how to convince and prove to employers that you have the competencies they need. This can sometimes be difficult or even laughable as alluded to previously with the reference to strategic agility. From my vantage point on my perch high above the noise, the competency nomenclature that is being churned out by HR departments is questionable. Come on—strategic agility? What is next? Accessible scalability? Okay, so I seem not to be a fan of competency-based systems. It is not that I am not a fan of competency-based systems; it is that I believe that the whole school of thought has been so twisted and reshaped to fit whatever meaning one wants to give it.

Unfortunately, dictionary definitions of the terms do not help much, because you must be able to speak the HR language, not the dictionary language, in order to get hired.

> If you research this topic you will find both *competence* and *competency* used interchangeably in the context of skills required for a job, but this approach is misleading.
>
> Using these terms, competence, competency, and competencies can only be effective in our context when there is one clear definition for each term and one that is acceptable to most employers at large.

Defining Competence, Competency, and Competencies

Competence refers to a potential ability and/or a capability to function in a given situation. *Competency* focuses on one's actual performance in a particular situation. This means that competence is required before one can expect to achieve competency.[4]

Definitions

Competence refers to potential ability or capability to perform.

Competency refers to actual performance.

Competencies are performance standards applied to a particular job, the group of skills, knowledge, style, and/or behaviors established by management (usually observed from those workers that demonstrate exemplary performance) that are required to perform the job at an acceptable level. (Some organizations prefer to use the descriptor "key characteristics required to be successful." Using this lingo, competencies are characteristics that individuals have and use in appropriate, consistent ways in order to achieve a desired performance. These characteristics include knowledge, skills, aspects of self-image, social motives, traits, thought patterns, mind-sets, and ways of thinking, feeling, and acting.

Competence and Finding the Right Job for You

In order to progress and take on new challenges one could argue that knowing your competence as well as your competency profile is just as important and maybe even more so. Knowing what you have the potential to do or have the ability to do is the key to understanding who you are and what you are good at, which then leads right into finding the right job that fits for you. This is why it is critical that you do the work in Chapter 2.

Much of the original competence theory was based on the tenet that the highest performers in any given area must get satisfaction through the fulfillment of personal needs. These needs I refer to as driving forces. This supports the central position of the book that in order to excel at your profession you need to be well matched, in terms of skills, behavior, knowledge, style, but most importantly interest and the fact that the job fulfills your driving forces or needs. Otherwise the pressure and stress of being mismatched leads to physical and emotional breakdown.

The Critical Stuff

We will address:

- The structure of an effective competency-based chronological resume and competency-based functional resume.
- How to decipher the corporate-speak in most job descriptions today so you can write a competency-based resume that gets picked.
- Understanding the use of action verbs when writing competency-based accomplishment statements.

Some of you may want to skip this chapter—I urge you not to do so. If you feel you know it all, at least review the critical items checklist to double-check your resume for all the key components. When my clients tell me they do not need their resume rewritten, I have them review the critical items list. Invariably they come back with something like, "Can you look my resume over, please?"

Critical Items Checklist

- **Content:** It is all about the content, not just about style and format.
- **Less is more:** Don't give everything away in the resume—just enough to whet the appetite in order for them to invite you for an in-person interview.
- **Accomplishments:** Focus on your accomplishments, not on your responsibilities and duties.
- **Keywords:** Most resumes are never reviewed by humans, especially when it comes to larger corporations. You must have the right keywords in order for your resume to be selected by the computer screening system, the ATS, for further review by a human. The higher the correlation of keywords in your resume to keywords in the job posting, the higher you rank in the initial screening. If you do not have most of the keywords in your resume, your resume does not go to the top of the ranking. You may be the perfect person for the job, but unfortunately without the correct keywords you are SOL.

➡ **Getting an interview:** Keywords get your resume selected by the computer for review by a human. The competencies supported by your *accomplishments* get the human reviewer to contact you for an in-person interview or a telephone screen.

➡ **Target your resume:** Ideally, customize your resume for every position you apply for by using the right keywords and accomplishments that demonstrate the key competencies needed by the employer or the ones you anticipate the decision-maker you are targeting will eventually need based on your research.

➡ **Competencies:** For your purposes, the competencies required for the job are usually in the job description under "Competencies" or under the usual headings, Qualifications, Skills, Requirements, or Background. If there is no current posting because no current opening exists, search for older job descriptions using your now-superior Google search skills.

➡ **Synergy:** Review the employer's Website and determine what values, and what functional and core competencies, are important. Demonstrate similar competencies in your resume.

➡ **Resumes:** Have two resumes—one designed for ATS and another for direct marketing to humans.

➡ **Brief and concise:** Remember that the word *résumé* is a French word meaning "to summarize," so make it brief and concise. Two pages are usually sufficient; three to four pages if you have publications and/or presentations you want to include. A one-page resume is commonplace today for executives and managers.

➡ **Focus the resume:** If you have everything but the kitchen sink scattered throughout your resume with little structure, you are inviting a "You're out of here" response. Most importantly, this reflects the fact you cannot communicate and organize your thoughts effectively. Who wants to hire someone with those competencies? Focus on key competencies that demonstrate the ability to meet a specific need and target a specific job.

➡ **Job title:** Make sure you use a job title that is used universally. Some employers have distinctive job title nomenclature. If that is the case at your employer, use a title like "manager of accounting" rather than your company-specific title of "head honcho of dollars."

➜ **What job do you want?** It is always important to tell the potential employer clearly, by including it on the resume, what job you would be well suited for and/or interested in. This is especially true for larger companies. If you let employers guess, *they won't.* Do not rely exclusively on a cover letter, because often cover letters are never read by a human or even entered into the tracking system. Indicate in the Profile or Objective the job title and the company you are applying to by name; this way they do not think you are fishing for a job but are really interested and took the time to research the employer.

➜ **Action verbs and words:** Stay away from statements like "I was responsible for...." or "I have experience with...." Replace them with the action words in Table 6.1.

➜ **No "I":** "I" is implied in each statement. For example, "I contributed to..." becomes "Contributed to...."

➜ **Readability:** Avoid giving the reviewer a headache. Let the resume breathe; make sure you leave space. A crammed resume is hard to read.

➜ **ProfessionaliBrand:** If you have developed a Professional Internet Brand, you must make sure your resume is consistent and in sync with it. An employer will Google you and check you out on the Internet, including social sites such as LinkedIn, Facebook, and others, and discrepancies will hurt you. Most employers are seeking technically and social media-savvy personnel. Therefore, an Internet presence is a must for all professionals. (Chapter 7 deals with ProfessionaliBranding in detail.)

➜ **Check out your personal brand or inadvertent iBrand—or your Internet footprint:** Your resume selection in many cases invites an automatic Internet or Google check by the employer (91 percent are Googling[5]). If your Internet footprint has to be cleaned up, take the steps necessary to have the offending items removed by contacting the specific Webmaster who controls the Website where the offending information is located and ask to have it removed. If need be, petition Google by using Google Webmaster Central. Click on "help center" and you should see "Need to remove content from Google search results? Here's how." Go to *www.transitiontohired.com/resources* for more information and a list of do-it-yourself services. It is difficult to have things removed once posted, so don't drink and post. Make sure your inadvertent iBrand is in sync with your resume as well, because employers will find the discrepancies.

➨ **Grab attention quickly:** The human reviewers will be sifting through many resumes, and most just glance at a resume to find what they are looking for. If it does not jump out at them they pass. Make it easy on them. Use a billboard at the top of your resume. For example, a manufacturing engineer might have this just below her contact information:

MANUFACTURING ENGINEER—LEAN MANUFACTURING—BLACK BELT

➨ **Appropriate for level:** Make sure the resume looks professional and is appropriate for your career level, and the type of position you are applying for.

➨ **Local candidates preferred:** If you are focused on relocating to a specific geographical area use a local telephone number on your resume area that corresponds to the area code where the job is located. Many companies consider local candidates first and will only relocate a new employee if they must. The tighter the economy, the more they focus on local candidates. You can get a telephone number in the area code you want by using Skype or a similar service and just forward the calls to your phone. You can simply leave out the address from your resume and just include the targeted city and state or province. Your name, telephone number, and e-mail address would be at the top of your resume, and your targeted city and state. (Make sure if you have a LinkedIn profile that your information is consistent.) Better yet, get a temporary address in the city where you want to relocate and use it on your resume. You can use a mail service such as Mail Boxes Etc. to get an address. Change your box number to the word Suite. For example, "box 12" becomes "Suite 12." Avoid using a P.O. box. If you are asked where you live, do not lie. Simply indicate that you are relocating to the area.

➡ **E-mail:** Select an e-mail name that is professional—preferably your name. Avoid shocking e-mail addresses such as sexdog@ livesex.com. Cute names and shocking names do not belong on a resume unless you are applying for a creative position or are in the entertainment industry.

➡ **Font selection:** Select font style carefully—for readability. If your resume is going to be reviewed on a computer screen, use sans serif fonts (Arial, Verdana, Trebuchet, Century Gothic, or Tahoma); for a printed version, the one you bring to an interview, use serif fonts (Times New Roman, Georgia, Bookman, or Garamond).

➡ **Style:** When direct marketing or meeting with an employer in person, a printed PDF document looks better. Spend some time on formatting and the styling of your resume. Looks make a difference, so bring a good-looking, printed PDF version for your in-person interviews. Choose bright white quality paper, 100-percent cotton, and 24 pound paper. *Do not use recycled copy paper.* Make sure the resume reflects how you look. If you are dressed sharply and your printed resume is ratty-looking, this will kill your image.

➡ **Professional resume services:** Avoid professional resume services at first. Your resume should be written by you. Put the time into crafting the resume yourself as it will help you during interviews. If you want to have it checked and tweaked by a professional resume service, choose a service wisely and get references.

➡ **Be truthful:** The repercussions of even small fibs can be very damaging to your reputation and can lead to a loss of employment at a future date when you are found out. The safe practice is to assume they will find out and you will get fired.

➡ **Proofread and review:** Have your resume proofread by someone who is good at grammar and editing, and make sure all spelling mistakes are corrected. Secondly, have it reviewed by someone who is competent in your job function. In most cases this means having two different people correct and review your resume.

GETTING PREPARED

It's not rocket science! I know how you feel after reading the resume information; you are thinking that having sinus surgery without anesthesia, performed by a blind surgeon using a harpoon, would be more fun. (I have nothing against blind surgeons; rather it is the choice of instrument that concerns me.)

Relax! Chill! Deep breaths. You can get through this! You are starting to think this is too much work and you want to dust off the old resume. Forget about it! *Stop!* Get rid of it, and start fresh. Follow the advice here, and the result will be a sparkling gem that will impress and get you to the top of the human resources' or hiring manager's "to call" list.

THE IMPORTANCE OF ACTION VERBS

Use action verbs and avoid a passive style of writing. For example: "I have experience with..." or "My responsibilities include..." Use action verbs, the more powerful the better.

Table 6.1: Action Verbs[6]

Research Skills	Technical Skills	Teaching Skills
clarified	assembled	adapted
collected	built	advised
critiqued	calculated	clarified
diagnosed	computed	coached
evaluated	designed	communicated
examined	devised	coordinated
extracted	engineered	developed
identified	fabricated	enabled
inspected	maintained	encouraged
interpreted	operated	evaluated
interviewed	overhauled	explained
investigated	programmed	facilitated
organized	remodeled	guided
reviewed	repaired	informed
summarized	solved	initiated
surveyed	trained	instructed
systematized	upgraded	persuaded
stimulated		set goals

Management Skills	Communication Skills	Clerical/Detailed Skills
administered	addressed	approved
analyzed	arbitrated	arranged
assigned	arranged	cataloged
attained	authored	classified
chaired	corresponded	collected
contracted	developed	compiled
consolidated	directed	dispatched
coordinated	drafted	executed
delegated	edited	generated
developed	enlisted	implemented
directed	formulated	inspected
evaluated	influenced	monitored
executed	interpreted	operated
improved	lectured	organized
increased	mediated	prepared
organized	moderated	processed
oversaw	motivated	purchased
planned	negotiated	recorded
prioritized	persuaded	retrieved
produced	promoted	screened
recommended	publicized	specified
reviewed	reconciled	systematized
scheduled	recruited	tabulated
strengthened	spoke	validated
supervised	translated	wrote

Financial Skills	Creative Skills	Helping Skills
administered	acted	assessed
allocated	conceptualized	assisted
analyzed	created	clarified
appraised	designed	coached
audited	developed	counseled
balanced	directed	
budgeted	established	demonstrated
calculated	fashioned	diagnosed
computed	founded	educated
developed	illustrated	expedited
forecasted	instituted	facilitated
managed	integrated	familiarized
marketed	introduced	guided
planned	invented	referred
projected	originated	rehabilitated
researched	performed	shaped
revitalized	planned	

How to Find the Right Keywords

Some of you may not realize it, but in most cases when applying to a large employer your resume will never be seen by a human until it is first selected by a computer. That is why it so important to understand the new hiring code. As mentioned previously, and this bears repeating, in order for your resume to get picked, the keywords on your resume get you selected by a computer for further review by a human. You need to make sure your resume is written with the applicant tracking system (ATS) selection process in mind.

Your goal is to get the right keywords in your resume that are pertinent to the job you are targeting. How do you know what keywords to put in your resume? The best place to find keywords is in existing job descriptions populating the Internet. The two methods I recommend are to use a visual keyword map and a word frequency counter. You can get access to both methods using Wordle (*www. wordle.net*), a great, free, Web-based tool.

Create a Word Cloud and Get a Visual Keyword Map for Your Resume

You may have seen something similar on Websites, usually in the margin, where you see a jumble of words. This is usually referred to as a tag cloud. By glancing at the cloud you can quickly ascertain the subject matter of the site or blog by the prominence of the keywords. I have adapted this same quick-scan approach to keyword research and selection for your resume.

A resume word cloud is a visual weighted depiction of the words from a document; the document consists of a number of similar job descriptions from different employers, where the weight or importance of a keyword is represented by font size or color. The clouds give greater prominence to keywords that appear more frequently in the source text. One of the great free tools available to you is Wordle. Here is an example of a how to create a Wordle keyword cloud for a manufacturing engineer in the automotive industry:

➤ Go to *www.indeed.com,* an automated job aggregator.

➤ Choose keywords that are representative of your profession (in this example, "Manufacturing Engineer Automotive") and enter these words in the search box. (Do not worry about entering a location.) Run the search.

➤ Select the first 10 job descriptions that are relevant.

➥ Copy and paste each job description, one after another (don't worry about how it looks) into *one* Microsoft Word or similar text-based, word-processing software program document, and save it as a plain-text document.

➥ Open your text file, select all, copy it, and go to Wordle.net.

➥ Paste your text in the window and click "Create."

➥ Review the Wordle you created. You can see what words are the keywords and therefore the most important words to include in your resume. Sometimes the result you will get will be pretty jumbled; you will need to adjust the Wordle output in order to review your keywords. You will find the Wordle toolbar (Edit, Language, Font, Layout, and Color) handy for this. Play around with it until you can read it properly.

Keyword Frequency

Although the visual cloud is a good start, I recommend that you go even deeper and review the specific word frequency or specific word count. This guarantees that you won't miss any valid keywords. Although this is tedious it allows you to review each keyword for actual numerical weighting as well as the opportunity to review each word in the document for acronyms, synonyms, or similar words so you do not miss an important keyword that may not have been depicted as important in the visual representation. This is one place where your employer research and employer list (which you created in Chapter 5) come in handy, because employers may use different names to represent the same meaning, such as *automotive*, *automobile*, *car*, *auto*, *vehicle*, and so on.

In order to get the word frequency count:

➥ Choose Language on the toolbar.

➥ Scroll to the bottom and click on "Show word counts."

➥ On the table that shows up, click on "Frequency" twice in order to list the words in order of most frequent to least frequent.

To guarantee being called for an interview, make sure the keywords are populated throughout your resume and their synonyms or equivalents are also included in your resume. You now have one of the most powerful tools to make sure your resume is the one that gets picked. You will rank high in resume database searches and get your resume put on the "to call" list.

What Competencies Should Your Resume Include?

For the purposes of building a resume that gets picked you need to understand two basic classifications of competencies:

1. Those identified, cherished, and valued by the organization or corporation as a whole (core competencies), and
2. Those required at the job-specific functional level (functional competencies).

First understand that theoretically each organization or corporation should have a core competence, and the whole idea of competencies requirements flows down from that core competence. For example, Microsoft has the core competence of designing office software products that are user-friendly and Federal Express has a core competence in logistics and customer service. In order for a corporation as a whole to realize and be recognized for their core competence and gain market advantage or dominance, a set of shared competencies are required from, or need to be developed in, every employee across the organization.

> This set of universal and organization-wide competencies defined at the corporate level is often referred to as core competencies.

For resume design purposes you need to retain the following about competencies:

- Core competencies are the competencies defined across the organization.
- Individual job-specific competencies are skills, knowledge, qualifications, and behavioral traits required to fulfill a particular job function within the organization.

If job-specific competencies are not spelled out under a heading called "competencies" in a job description, then look for the tried and true headlines commonly found in job descriptions, requirements, qualifications, skills, and background. For example, a hardware engineer requires specific skills, qualifications, knowledge, and behavioral traits or specific competencies to be a good at his job. Here is an example of competencies in a job description for a controls hardware design engineer[7]:

Competencies

➡ Technical Competencies

   ⇨ Autocad

   ⇨ E-plan (preferred)

   ⇨ Microsoft Office competent

   ⇨ Microsoft project competent

➡ Core Competencies

   ⇨ Initiative

   ⇨ Results orientation

   ⇨ Decision making

   ⇨ Ability to analyze

   ⇨ Organizing and quality orientation

   ⇨ Communication skills

   ⇨ Team player

   ⇨ Ability to work under minimum supervision

If you want to develop a resume you can use over and over, then you need to identify the competencies valued by most corporations as a whole and the job-specific competencies most sought after for your job function throughout your list of target employers.

Ideally, when applying directly to an employer it is best to customize your resume to reflect the needs of the employer. To find the relevant competencies sought after for the type of job you are seeking, review a number of job descriptions that are specific to your job function or specialty. Only include competencies on your resume if you can demonstrate that you indeed possess those competencies. Use a job description aggregator or search spider such as Indeed.com to search for job descriptions you can review. It is also important to include some valued core competencies on your resume—those expected or required from the employers on your target list. Find these by searching the Websites of the employers on your list to uncover their list of core competencies.

CORE COMPETENCIES MOST VALUED BY CORPORATIONS

One way to develop a one-size-fits-all, competency-based resume is to figure out what core competencies are valued by the majority of large corporations in your industry that you have identified as prime targets. You can do this by researching each employer's site on your list to find their list of core competencies.

Alternatively, you can take a blanket approach and cover the core competencies most valued by companies in America and the UK identified by Robin Kessler and Linda A. Strasburg in *Competency-Based Resumes.*) (This list has been modified.)

List of Most Valued Core Competencies[8]

→ Results orientation

→ Initiative

→ Impact and influence

→ Team orientation

→ Communication

→ People management

→ Customer focus

→ Problem-solving

→ Planning and organization

→ Technical skills

→ Leadership

→ Business awareness

→ Decision-making

→ Analytical thinking

→ Conceptual thinking

→ Information-seeking

→ Integrity

→ Organizational awareness

The idea of the one-size-fits-all resume is to build your resume in order to demonstrate the competencies that are specific to your job function as well as some of the competencies coveted, listed here, by most corporations. You only have a limited amount of space on a resume, so start with the job-specific functions because these will often be duplicated in the core competencies list.

Conduct research on the job-specific competencies required for the job function you are targeting and make a list. Remember, however, that the most effective way to ensure that your resume gets picked is to customize it for every submission you make.

THE IMPORTANCE OF ACCOMPLISHMENTS

The resume is not a story about your responsibilities or duties. It is not just a job description. It is about the facts: What did you do? What did you accomplish? In today's job market competencies supported by accomplishments are the focus. Simply listing a bunch of competencies on a resume without any supporting accomplishments just does not cut it.

An accomplishment is defined using metrics, such as dollars, percentages, and time saved. For the most puritan competency evangelists, if an accomplishment can't be measured it does not exist.

Usually the words and keywords that will get your resume selected by the HR software are related to the job-specific competencies—the functional parts of your job—and, as previously stated, sometimes these are still represented under headings such as technical skills and qualifications.

> The keyword selection by the ATS is not what gets you the interview. In order to get an interview you need to impress a person. You impress a person with your accomplishments.

It is also good to know that this work will help you with interviews because in a competency-based interview system the key selection factor is how well you can demonstrate or prove your competencies with supporting accomplishments.

Use the following structure when formulating your accomplishment statements or bullet points. The result is impactful.

PAR

Problem: What was the problem (situation)?

Action: What action did you take?

Result: What was the result?

You can vary this approach. If you want to grab the employer's attention, state the result first and use the Results-Action-Problem (RAP) format.

Examples:

➡ Delivered an 80% ROI on new memberships by hiring an independent telephone marketing company to reverse declining memberships and increase membership growth. Marketing drive increased paid memberships from 200 to 533 within 3 months of taking leadership of the department—setting a company record.

Note: The accomplishment statement above could be used to demonstrate the following competencies: initiative, results orientation, and problem-solving.

Note: Begin each accomplishment statement with an action verb and make sure it is a powerful action verb.

➡ Contributed technical input to the railway signalling project that increased traffic flow capacity by 22%.

Write a list of accomplishment statements related to each job you have had. Jot them down for now and make a comprehensive list. Make sure that you quantify the accomplishment using dollars, percentages, and time.

Bringing it All Together: Writing Your Masterpiece

Your resume needs to answer the following:

1. What is your Sustainable Competitive Advantage over your competition?

2. What are your competencies?

   a. What are your skills?

      i. Present your functional skills: instruments, machines, processes, and/or software you have used.

      ii. Provide your industry keywords, lingo, and buzzwords.

   b. What is your knowledge?

      i. Remember it encompasses everything: information you have gathered, understanding of cultures, languages, challenges, activities, places, ideas, and anything else you can think of that may be remotely valuable. It includes special knowledge of industries, competitive knowledge, product positioning, ability to call on your network for help, ability as a speaker, presenter, or trainer.

      ii. Education and training: consider all that is relevant to the dream job you seek.

  c. What is your style?

      i. Consider your strengths, work style, thinking style, stamina/resilience, communication style, and management style or subordinate style (whichever is appropriate).

3. What accomplishments have you achieved that will prove that you have the right stuff for the job?

  a. In answering this question, consider PAR. We are not talking about golf here but rather Problem-Action-Results. What problems have you been given or have you identified? What action did you take? What were the results? You need to quantify these results where possible.

4. What have you done with respect to influencing the bottom line?

  a. Consider that everyone is hired in a business to do one of three things: to make money, to save money, or to do both for their employer. You need to point out what, where, and how you have done this. Again, you need to quantify these results.

5. What is your work history?

  a. Dates: include month and year.

  b. Employer: name and one-line description about the company or division if not well known.

  c. Job Title: Make sure you use a universally recognized job title, not something obtuse such as "talent acquisition" (instead use "recruiter").

SUMMARY OR PROFILE

Every resume greatly benefits from a profile or summary. This is the section at the beginning of your resume that, combined with your billboard, will grab the reviewer's attention. The profile section that you will create will "sell" the hiring manager and will convey a powerful message in order to compel him to read more. It is a matter of personal preference which heading title you use (summary or profile); I prefer profile because it has a human connotation to it.

Why is the profile so important? Should you fail to entice the reader, your resume becomes recycling paper. Of course, if your resume is in a digital format, it could be screened by a person afflicted by that dreaded disease—"deletiosis"—and all that hard work will be turned into a mishmash of bits and bytes. Can you feel the pain of all your hard work being treated so harshly because you skimped on your profile? Simply follow the step-by-step process to a winning profile.

The profile needs to scream out:

➤ This is who I am.

➤ This is what I do and/or did (hard facts) and/or can do for you.

➤ This is what I know.

➤ This is what I specialize in.

➤ This is what makes me special.

➤ This is my style.

➤ This is a hard fact that will make you take notice.

You have already done most of the work required by developing your SCA. I would like to show you how easy it is for you now to take that information and develop your own profile for your resume. In order to do that, let's use an SCA as an example to demonstrate the process of creating a profile. Our target position is a director of new business development for a personnel recruitment firm. Here is your reward for doing your due diligence and getting your SCA done: a template so you can develop your profile, quick-lickety-split!

Developing Your Profile Using a Profile Template

First, retrieve your SCA and keep it handy, because you will be mining it for the content of your profile.

I am a successful entrepreneur with extensive experience in the International Recruitment business, supported by the fact that I have won many awards for outstanding achievement in this field. I am a coach who has trained and mentored many to achieve success in business. I am a burgeoning writer with a zany style, and I am extremely passionate about writing. I am a dominant leader of leaders, with great vision, and the power of great influence over others. I am at my best when faced with troubleshooting, or finding solutions to problems by using my strategic thinking style—that is, my instinctual ability to predict upcoming events. I am extremely

*creative and have a wild imagination that gives me a gift for innovation. Manage-
ment is not a strength but when the situation requires, I am a macro manager who
empowers my people to take risks, and to learn by doing. My greatest weakness is I
am not good with detail. As a leader, I am confident in the face of adversity, and I
get my followers to "loosen up" by making the work environment fun. What I espouse
and live by is "You can do anything you want to do; all you have to do is do it. Do
what you love and the money will come."*

Use the following template to create your own version. Simply replace the
underlined words with your own appropriate words from your SCA.

A/an(personality trait) (your title or job category) with proven success over
(number of relevant years of experience) years in (your specialty) the (your
industry) industry. Recognized for/as (strength or accomplishment). Can be
counted on to (your style, your interpersonal style, your work style). (Add a
hard fact or impressive achievement.)

Here is the profile as a result of using the content from the prior SCA
example and plugging it into the template:

An influential and successful entrepreneur with proven success over 23
years in international personnel recruitment in the pharmaceutical industry.
Recognized as a leader of leaders, who is creative, is innovative, and has a well-
developed strategic thinking style. Can be counted on to train, develop, and
retain staff by empowering them to take risks and by making the work environment fun. Built start-up into reputable international recruitment company and
drove sales to over $2M within 5 years.

Note the focus on competencies, leadership style, action verbs, and an accomplishment in the profile.

Use the template as a framework to get started. There is no hard and fast
rule that your profile must use the words in the template. Make your profile
your own.

When customizing your resume for a particular job and employer, you
need to focus your profile on the competencies required for that specific job
description and the core competencies required by that specific employer.

It does not have to be perfect the first go-around. Just get it down, then
edit until you have a powerful profile.

RESUME STYLES THAT GET YOU HIRED

As mentioned earlier, the typical approach to writing a resume is to outline your skills, background, accomplishments, and work history in a chronological order, and hope that these match up with what the employer is looking for. A much better approach, and this bears repeating, is to figure out the employer's core competencies and the functional or job-specific competencies, and tailor a resume that matches the employer's needs. The resume types that best accomplish this are the competency-based chronological resume and the competency-based functional resume. Following are examples of actual resumes.

Competency-Based Chronological Resume

ItsMe

127 Give Me a Great Job Rd, Hope, TX 12345

Home: 123-456-7890

Cell: 098-765-4321

E-mail: ItsMe@BioanalyticalScientist.com

BIOANALYTICAL SCIENTIST-LEADERSHIP-INNOVATIVE

PROFILE

A pragmatic scientist, with over 10 years of proven success in medicinal chemistry, analytical chemistry, protein biochemistry, and biophysics with a focus on bioanalytical method development and validation in the pharmaceutical industry. Recognized for ability to streamline processes, cut time to delivery of projects, and save money for the company, as demonstrated by a $200,000 costs savings.

Problem-solver who analyzes and then initiates and implements creative resolutions to achieve expected end results. Can be counted on to lead and raise the level of commitment, sharing of knowledge, and productivity within dedicated work teams as demonstrated by collaborations with world-leading academic laboratories. Scientific peer community recognition through publications and presentations at industry conferences.

Agilent LC/MSD 1100, LC-ESI-TOF, Voyager MALDI_TOF, Thermo Electron LTQ-Orbitrap, Vantage and Water's Micromass LC-MS/MS

EMPLOYMENT HISTORY

2002–present   Principal Scientist, The Lab, Somewhere, PA, USA

➤ Delivered projects on time using current analytical methodologies for quantitation, characterization, trace level impurity identification associated with bio-molecules (Various HPLC and LC/MS, LS/MS-MS systems).

➤ Reduced the cost of analytical method development by 10% compared to 2007, and reduced the time to delivery by 30% by empowering my team to experiment, take risks, and implement their own creative solutions.

➤ Saved $200,000 for the company by improving existing methods, thereby avoiding the need for performing new development projects. Satisfied client needs on time and within budget.

➤ Faced with a drastic downdraft in business and being instructed by management to prepare a list for layoffs, contacted my scientific network and secured $2M in new business, saving jobs and contributing significantly to the company's bottom line. As a result of initiative chosen as a contributor to the "inner management circle" of the company.

➤ Improved new method development process by training team members to share knowledge between each other. This has also led to the development of strong team cohesion where team members are proactive about volunteering to help others on the team.

➤ Applied FDA Guidance for the industry, and ICH Guidelines as they related to DS and DP characterization, control, and stability.

TECHNICAL SKILLS

Analytical techniques

➤ Chromatography (SEC, UPLC, HPLC). Experience in method development, validation, and their maintenance.

➤ Mass spectrometer (MALDI-TOF, ESI-TOF, LC-MS/MS). Familiar with Agilent LC/MSD 1100, LC-ESI-TOF, Voyager MALDI_TOF, Thermo Electron LTQ-Orbitrap, Vantage and Water's micromass LC-MS/MS.

Spectroscopy

➤ NMR (1D, 2D [DQF-COSY, TOCSY and NOESY]), UV-visible, Circular Dichroism, Fluorescence.

Biological assay

➤ Hemolytic assay (human RBCs), E.Coli, Staphylococcus, and Pseudomonas assay for screening wide array of antimicrobial peptides.

Synthetic, peptide, and combinatorial chemistry

➤ Synthesizing protected amino acids (side chain, N- and C-terminus protection), unusual amino acids, and other chemical modifications. Familiar with Boc, Z, and Fmoc chemistry.

Computer, informatics, and modeling

➤ Familiar with PC, MAC, UNIX, and MSDOS platforms, FELIX and SPARKY software for 2D NMR data processing and analysis, basic knowledge in structural modeling software like INSIGHTII.

EDUCATION

1998–2002 Ph.D. University of Universities, Where it Is, USA

List of publications and presentations available on request.

Competency-Based Functional Resume

ItsMe

127 Give Me a Great Job Rd, Hope, TX 12345

Home: 123-456-7890

Cell: 098-765-4321

E-mail: ItsMe@BioanalyticalScientist.com

RESULTS FOCUS-LEADERSHIP-INNOVATIVE-PROFESSIONAL NETWORKING

PROFILE

A pragmatic leader, with over 10 years of proven success in leading and supervising scientific teams. Recognized for ability to streamline processes, cut time to delivery of projects, and save money, as demonstrated by a $200,000 costs savings. Problem-solver who analyzes and then initiates and implements creative resolutions to achieve expected end results. Can be counted on to lead and raise the level of commitment, sharing of knowledge, and productivity within dedicated work teams. Value collaboration and professional networking to speed up delivery of projects. Well-developed writing and presentation skills as demonstrated by scientific peer community recognition publications and presentations at industry conferences.

INNOVATION, COST CUTTING, AND SUPERVISION

Reduced the cost of analytical method development by 10% compared to 2007, and reduced the time to delivery by 30%, by empowering my team to run with the projects.

INITIATIVE, NETWORKING, INNOVATION, AND BUSINESS DEVELOPMENT

Faced with a drastic downdraft in business and being instructed by management to prepare a list for layoffs, I contacted my network and secured $2M in new business, saving jobs and contributing significantly to the company's bottom line. As a result of my initiative, I have been chosen as a contributor to the "inner management circle" of the company.

Technical Skills and Results Focus

Delivered projects on time using current analytical methodologies for quantitation, characterization, trace level impurity identification associated with bio-molecules (various HPLC and LC/MS, LS/MS-MS systems).

COLLABORATION AND LEADERSHIP

Improved new method development process by training team members to share knowledge between each other. This has also led to the development of strong team cohesion, where team members are proactive about volunteering to help others on the team.

SCIENTIFIC INSTRUMENTS AND ANALYTICAL CHEMISTRY

➔ Chromatography (SEC, UPLC, HPLC). Experience in method development, validation, and their maintenance.

➔ Mass spectrometer (MALDI-TOF, ESI-TOF, LC-MS/MS). Familiar with Agilent LC/MSD 1100, LC-ESI-TOF, Voyager MALDI_TOF, Thermo Electron LTQ-Orbitrap.

EMPLOYMENT

Principal Scientist, The Lab, Somewhere, PA, USA
Education
Ph.D. University of Universities, Where it Is
Publications and presentations **available on request.**

DOES YOUR RESUME PASS THE "GET HIRED" TEST?

After you have written your competency-based resume, test it. Will the employer get answers to: "What results will you produce for me and what transformation to my company, department, or customers can I expect?" and "Why are you qualified to deliver these transformations and results?" You will be customizing your resume as a result of what you learn in the upcoming chapters.

Chapter 7

Be Irresistible Through ProfessionaliBranding

"IN THE END, YOU MAKE YOUR REPUTATION AND YOU HAVE YOUR SUCCESS
BASED UPON CREDIBILITY AND BEING ABLE TO PROVIDE PEOPLE WHO ARE RE-
ALLY HUNGRY FOR INFORMATION WHAT THEY WANT."
—BRIT HUME[1]

What if you never, ever had to search for another job again but still had the
luxury of being offered a new job? When I speak to professionals about their
job search and I ask them if they enjoy it, the answer is always a resounding
no! They dread it. They also share with me their fears of job insecurity. By now
you have come to realize job security is no longer a reality, nor are counting on
an employer and a traditional job search a good way to protect your income
or provide security for your family. Most of you hate the traditional job-search
process and the consensus among professionals is that it is trying, tiring, de-
meaning, depressing, and frustrating.

> Thankfully the new job search is not about searching for work but rather being constantly proactive by creating an irresistible offer online that employers are attracted to and are compelled to act on. It is about selecting what fits for you, not about fitting in!

The explosion in Web technology has given every professional easy and affordable channels with literally global access to attract employers and great job opportunities. Conversely, it has also given employers incredible tools to find you, track you, and keep tabs on you.

In the Web 2.0[2] world it is not so much "who you know" but who knows about you, what they are saying about you, and if that information about you is shared. The way people and employers who don't know you get to know you today and form an opinion about you as a professional is through the message you promote on the Internet, inadvertently or purposefully, and more importantly through what others say about you. Nowhere is this phenomenon of social proof and conforming to others' opinions more prevalent than on the Web, where social proof through social signals (likes, +1s, number of viewer counts, and so forth) and social media rule today. On the Web, for example, the collective opinion of consumers through product reviews, thumbs up or thumbs down, will influence most people's decision to buy or not to buy a product. Alternatively, you can think of social proof as social influence or social conformity. In *Social Psychology*, the authors say, "We conform because we believe that other's interpretation of an ambiguous situation is more accurate than ours and will help us choose an appropriate course of action."[3] Social proof is often also referred to as "herd mentality."

A great example of this herd mentality is when I started my first really successful business: Brats and Dogs, a hot dog cart that sold high-quality bratwurst. To grab market share from the other vendors when I first arrived on the scene, I offered my friends free food to line up and then hang out around the cart. Invariably this attracted attention, and I was able to build buzz and a steady clientele. Passersby would see the line and be compelled to check it out, and by delivering great unique content—a handmade bratwurst, instead of a plain hot dog like every other vendor did—I captured the high-end market as well as the low-end market for hot dogs, because clients assumed I also had higher-quality hot dogs. I built a flourishing business that paid my way through university.

This is true for hot dog carts as well as on the Web. On the Web and in social networking people count on the collective opinion of others to form their opinion of you. The collective opinion of support, dissatisfaction, or ambivalence about a professional is communicated through "like" buttons, +1s, comments, the re-sharing of content, and public endorsements. The Internet and the Web have provided you with unparalleled reach and power to sway the opinion about you as a professional. How to get the phenomenon of social proof or social influence to bolster your professional image is what ProfessionaliBranding is all about. Get a few to notice, and others will notice and clamor to join in. As long as you provide a steady stream of enticing content, employers and decision-makers will take notice and come to check you out. Yes, everyone can do it! It is also about Web 3.0—the ability of employers to be able to track you through what you think is your so-called private information by the footprint you leave on the Internet. Web 3.0 exists because sophisticated services exist that monitor social media networks like Facebook, LinkedIn, and Twitter for any relevant information on a chosen topic, and then these services' robust algorithm filters the data from several public sources and cross-references them with "user name," e-mail addresses, and the like that you use or have used to identify you and build a "real time" profile on you right down to, in some cases, being able to physically locate you by GPS through your phone.

The Be Irresistible, ProfessionaliBranding formula is quite simple:

➥ Outline your SCA.

➥ Create your online identity associated with your SCA and establish your credibility.

➥ Promote your identity and credibility by linking it to your social media/networking efforts.

➥ Build connections, get noticed, develop fans and endorsers (social proof), get hired, and be continuously proactive about job search in order to secure your income.

➥ Protect your privacy.

PROFESSIONALIBRAND VS. PERSONALIBRAND

The information about you on the Internet, inadvertent or not, the information you leave about you, the information others leave about you, the information that you point out as being important about you, the information tied to you and your profession, the information about your interactions socially, is in fact your personal brand—or your Personal Internet Brand (Personali-Brand).

> Your employability has become the sum total of everything you say and do on the Internet, or, in other words, your employability is as good as your PersonaliBrand.

On October 3, 2011, Kashmir Hill, who bills herself as a "privacy pragmatist" and is part of *Forbes'* staff, reported on Forbes.com that "Reppler...recently commissioned a new survey of 300 hiring types to see how they're using Facebook, Twitter, LinkedIn, Craigslist, Tumblr, MySpace, et al. to screen candidates: 91% of them are doing social networking screens of job applicants."[4] The Reppler survey also pointed out that 69 percent of those surveyed admitted to rejecting a candidate based on what they found through their social networking sleuthing efforts. The good news is the message is getting through about the importance of a professional image on the Internet, because, when asked how often social networking profiles were a factor to a candidate getting hired, the answer turned out to be very positive: "That turned out to be the case for 68% of them."[5]

Even the "biggies" are chiming in on the importance of your "digital cred" with their own studies. Microsoft reports in a study that 70 percent of HR professionals in the United States and 41 percent in the United Kingdom will disqualify an applicant based on what they dig up about the person on the Internet. According to this same Microsoft study, even more importantly, Internet reputation can also have a positive effect: In the United States, 86 percent of HR professionals (and at least two thirds of those in the UK and Germany) stated that a positive online reputation influences the candidate's application to some extent; almost half stated that it does so to a great extent.[6]

This is powerful stuff.

Understanding the following distinction is critical to building an irresistible offer; if left unmanaged your PersonaliBrand will become your ProfessionaliBrand.

> Your Professional Internet Brand, or ProfessionaliBrand, is the opinion others have of you as a *professional* based on what they find out about you on the Internet, regardless of its source or intent.

As the Microsoft study and the Reppler survey clearly point out, it is critical for you to separate your PersonaliBrand from your ProfessionaliBrand.

Take notice of this critically important development that affects your privacy. In June 2011, the Federal Trade Commission in the United States gave its blessing to Social Intelligence Corporation to scour social media and Internet sites to dig up dirt on employees and job applicants.[7]

The trend is now for employers to do background checks by checking out your Internet footprint as well as your Internet crumbs. I call "crumbs" the little stuff—things you don't even know you left behind, such as a link between the different user names you use, or the information about your attendance at a professional conference, or the fact that you coach Little League baseball. Most sites share user name information and behavior—not actual identity—however, Social Intelligence can join the dots, identify you as the owner of the different user names, and feed it up on a platter to your potential or future employer.

> Establishing your "digital cred" or ProfessionaliBrand has never been more important. Equally important is protecting your privacy in the new Web 3.0 world because employers are spying on you!

Social media and recruiting are matches made in heaven when one considers that networking is the best tool for finding work. Capitalizing on social media is becoming the recruiting method of choice for employers. The professionals that *get it* will have a distinct advantage over those that are still lying in the shadows with respect to creating or encouraging positive social signals about their value as potential employees. As technology is now being developed to help employers in harvesting and managing all the information about you on the Web and also tracking you (Web 3.0), as well as the social signals about potential employees, ProfessionaliBranding is critical for all professionals if they want to get noticed, get pursued, and guarantee their employment now and for years to come. New services and consultants specializing in and having the ability to capitalize on social media are popping up to help put order and manageability into Recruiting 3.0. Recruiting 3.0 is a new phenomenon precipitated by advances in technology as well as the war for talent being conducted globally. Web 2.0 was all about relationships; Recruiting 3.0 through Web 3.0 is all about how employers and others (background check firms) are tracking what you consider to be your private information trail, which is really not so private. Your trail influences your reputation and the signals you leave are being exploited for data gathering by employers. Scary, I must admit.

Globalization is forcing companies to be more aggressive in recruiting the best talent, wherever it may be in the world, and technology gives companies great recruiting breath as well as the ability to tap into that talent and its productivity without having to relocate professionals. Case in point: Many of my service providers for my businesses work in foreign countries and deliver excellent work for me and our team. I found them through filtering social media data.

Recruiting 3.0 is about the best companies using the best recruiting practices to secure the best talent by analyzing the social signals about everything about you, including what you love, what you hate, where you shop, what sites you visit, what you say, and what others say about you. You need to realize that in the new Web 3.0 world you are being "tagged" everywhere you go, offline and online, and systems have been setup to select from the collective noise, by crunching all the data, the best potential employees from anywhere in the world to actively pursue. By being able to tap into a global pool and select the best employees with the best match in competencies, Recruiting 3.0–enlightened companies are maintaining their strategic advantage over their competitors. Recruiting is no longer limited to going after professionals who signal their interest in new employment, but rather, in theory every professional that has a footprint on the Internet is fair game. The noise these employers must filter through is all the information about all the potential employees, be they actively looking or not, throughout the world. Search and the analysis and management of this data are key to the success of any recruiting strategy, but also the filtering, capture, and analysis of social signals/data are key best practices in recruiting today.

The new job-search methodology for employers is *everyone* is a potential employee, if and only if employers can find you on the Internet. No longer is recruitment at the employer level focused on professionals who are actively seeking work. Applicants do not matter as much anymore; the race is on by employers to find and identify the right candidates. Will you be a proactive candidate by developing a strong ProfessionaliBrand, or will you rely on being an applicant?

Just a few years ago the great advantages headhunters had over employers was their access to professionals who were hard to come by, the so-called "passive candidate" who was employed and not actively searching for work. Now most employers have replaced their dependence on, or limited their need for, headhunters by having access to a large pool of proactive candidates that they can tap into directly with sophisticated search tools, active social media strategies, and referral reward programs, as well as sophisticated data capture and analysis tools. The competencies of the new recruiter in the Recruiting 3.0 world include the ability to use sophisticated tools and strategies to uncover the best candidates through social networking and search as well as promote his company's recruiting brand to specific target communities of professionals. Employers need to develop their own recruiting brands just as professionals need to develop their own ProfessionaliBrand.

Fortune 500 companies are realizing the potential of Recruiting 3.0 in a big way and are integrating social media, networking, and referral tools combined with reward systems into their recruiting strategy. Case in point is Mesh-Hire. Here is how this service geared to employers describes its service on their Website: "MeshHire is a cloud-based referral recruiting and marketing platform designed to help recruiters and human resources professionals create and manage their Talent Referral Network across social networking Websites like Facebook, LinkedIn, and Twitter. MeshHire serves worldwide customers from start-ups to Fortune 500 companies, providing the most comprehensive social and referral recruitment solution in the industry."[8]

Services like MeshHire are truly changing the landscape of recruiting. Recruiting 3.0 has truly arrived. When you analyze Sarah E. Needleman's *Wall Street Journal* article "Recruiting 3.0: Web Advances Change the Landscape,[9] you clearly come to the conclusion that Recruiting 3.0 was only in its infancy in 2008. Recruiting 3.0 has matured and is a force that has to be recognized by professionals because it combines the power of numerous channels including the Web, e-mail, social networking, blogs, audio, podcasting, video, live streaming, video conferencing and video interviewing, broadcasting, social media data management and mining, online referral reward systems, and the power of stealth tracking and the power of search to complete the 3.0 recruiting stew. It should be noted that the information employers garner from these channels as well as the connections they make online are the precursors to an employer taking the relationship offline and meeting with you. Even this step of meeting with potential employees is beginning to be relegated more and more to video interviews. Most eye-opening, however, is that some employee–employer relationships are *truly* happening virtually.

Work interactions are happening in a truly virtual world such as Second Life where IBM workers interface as Avatars.[10] Even interviews are being conducted "Avatar to Avatar," as reported in the *Wall Street Journal,* such that company Avatar representatives (from Microsoft, Verizon, and others) are interviewing Avatar candidates for jobs in real space[11] (sounds weird to have to say "real space" to identify terra firma). To avoid being left behind, you need to accept that job search has come a long way from simply attaching your resume to an e-mail and sending it out. Okay, maybe Second Life was or is a bit ahead of its time and Avatar interviews are not catching on, but the fact that employers are experimenting with all types of new technologies just means that they will continue to do so, and you must be able to differentiate between what is a fad and what is a trend and take the necessary action. Some of the best jobs in the world may no longer be available to you unless you embrace becoming a Recruiting 3.0–friendly candidate through ProfessionaliBranding.

In order to guarantee your income, the facts clearly require a new job search strategy. This is why I created the concept of the ProfessionaliBrand to differentiate it from your PersonaliBrand. As you now can clearly understand managing your professional image online and ProfessionaliBranding are critical to your employability. Influencing the professional message about you so others don't create one for you is also critical to your future success in getting hired. How do you determine what message your ProfessionaliBrand should clearly communicate? Well, that is easy. You have already done all the work. As you determined in Chapter 2, your Sustainable Competitive Advantage (SCA) is equal to "Professional Brand You."

As you have now come to realize, a ProfessionaliBrand that is managed, can help you; left unmanaged it can hurt you, and having none leaves employers to form their own opinion of your personality, sociability, and technical savvy. Many employers want technically savvy professionals and they are using Recruiting 3.0 as the vehicle to find them, so if they cannot find you online, they most likely will not be calling you.

> Your goal is to build a ProfessionaliBrand that is so compelling that it acts as an irresistible offer so that employers will find you and offer you jobs, so you never, ever have to look for a job ever again.

Developing a compelling ProfessionaliBrand is about announcing and promoting to the world the unique professional you, what you do, why you do it, and how you do it. It is about making your SCA come alive publicly by leaving an extended, impactful Internet footprint in an engaging manner so that it is viewed frequently. It is about telling the world's employers what you love to do and how you can make the world a better place by doing your best. It is about getting paid for doing what you love, doing what fits for you, and not compromising on your values and driving forces. It is about being open and flexible to entertain any offer where your uniqueness can benefit others. It is about being a proactive job searcher. It is akin to putting your job search on steroids, 24/7, each and every day, forever, without actually looking for a job but rather being open (proactive) to entertain offers. It is about making the on-line you so attractive that you become a candidate to those employers that are alerted to you rather than you having to chase jobs through the conventional applicant route.

ProfessionaliBranding is also about communicating a consistent and re-liable message throughout all your channels. Your channels include e-mail, LinkedIn profile, iResumePro with unique domain name, Internet video re-sume, social media sites, Facebook, Twitter, Google+, blog, and many others. Building an effective irresistible offer through ProfessionaliBranding takes time. It is like planting a seed: You need to find a spot, till the soil, water and enrich the soil, plant your seed, and then protect and provide for your seed and young plant before it turns into a viable and robust plant. You cannot expect to plant a seed today and harvest tomorrow. The same is true with developing your ProfessionaliBrand. The quicker you get started, the quicker you will reap the harvest of being offered jobs.

PROFESSIONALIBRANDING LEVELS

Level 1: The Must Level

- ➥ Discover your SCA—your unique you. Build your profile.

- ➥ Discover your keywords—the words that represent your profession.

- ➥ Write your competency-based resume.

- ➥ Google your name and/or find any traces of you on the Internet. Determine if damage control is needed. Correct if you can. (Check out Chapter 6 for more information, and use the service Reppler.com to clean up any messes.)

- ➥ Use your resume to develop your LinkedIn profile.

- ➥ Develop a keyword-rich LinkedIn profile.

➡ Use "Internet crumbs" to your advantage. Include your job title and place of work, and a Web-based e-mail address in all places where your name will show up on the Internet, conferences, professional directories, associations, sports event participation, and so forth.

Level 2: Irresistible Branding Level

➡ Select your keyword-rich domain name.

➡ Build a VisualCV. (See later in the chapter for more information.)

➡ Develop your resume Website (iResumePro) with your online competency-based resume.

➡ Develop an "e-mail resume button" and add it to your e-mail signature.

➡ Search engine optimize your iResumePro.

➡ Develop your iVideoResumePro and post it on your Website.

➡ Institute iBlitz17 (see the section later in chapter) social media strategy: LinkedIn, Facebook, Twitter.

➡ Create back links to your iResumePro by commenting on blog entries and leaving your iResumePro's URL to increase search engine ranking.

➡ Set up a CRM system and/or use JibberJobber, or categorize your networks. Tag your connections in LinkedIn or create Google circles. Provide compelling information directly to your networks through e-mail marketing, newsletters, white papers, or industry trends.

➡ Export your network contact lists from LinkedIn, Facebook, and so forth, and contact them through e-mail with compelling information/content.

➡ Set up a professional blog on your iResumePro Website. Tell the world what your SCA is by blogging.

➡ Set up your YouTube channel and post your resume video. Also post your iVideoResumePro on your Website without a YouTube link, because some employers do not have access to YouTube at work.

➡ Consider using TubeMogul to distribute your videos across different sites and increase your search engine findability. (Go to *www.transitiontohired.com/resources* for more information on using TubeMogul.)

→ Join Web-based communities relevant to your profession or the job you are interested in and become an active commenter or poster (not a pest).

At a minimum, every professional must attain a Level 1 Professionali-Brand. You reach the irresistible level once you complete Level 2. Do not be surprised if you begin to get offers before you complete Level 2.

I identify an additional level that is beyond the scope of this book as Level 3. It is what I call the Key Opinion Leader. If you would like to find out more go to *www.transitiontohired.com.* Of course there are many more initiatives at each level you can take because new sites and tools are mushrooming every day. Evaluate and use those that offer advantages to your ProfessionaliBranding strategy.

How Others Get to Know You

In order to thrive as a professional today you need to understand how ProfessionaliBranding is changing hiring and how employers are exploiting the shift to social networking for their benefit. Building a compelling professional image revolves around answering the question "Who are you?" not simply "What do you do?" Employers do not hire people based on what they do alone, but based on who they are. They only hire you if they feel they know you, like you, and trust you. There is no better way today to reach as many employers with a message that lets them get to know you, like you, and trust you than through the development, management, and promotion of your powerful ProfessionaliBrand—in other words, by making your professional Internet footprint easily findable by being a Recruiting 3.0-friendly candidate.

You want to build a ProfessionaliBrand in order to attract the right job for you by telling the world about your interests and passions; if you love what you do, you will do it well and be recognized for it, and your professional image will grow and be noticed. Who you are, what you love, and what you do best will be all over the Web, attracting recognition from others and interest from employers.

You may already be doing what you love, doing it well, and adding value to the world. However, you may not be promoting yourself on the Internet, and therefore not reaching the widest audience and the right employers who can help you touch more people with your unique competencies. You also may not be getting the recognition you deserve. Your job security may also be in question. Alternatively, you may not like the job you are doing now and want to change. By attracting a new employer and the right employer that shares a mutual vision with you and values your SCA greatly, you will be viewed as a candidate and be in a better bargaining position to get rewarded in ways that are more beneficial for you. These rewards can come from financial compensation or even non-financial rewards, such as flexible work hours and the like.

If you want to shift careers or employers all you have to do is promote your SCA. Start pursuing what you love and start promoting it on the Internet. Create a ProfessionaliBranding campaign to get you to where you want to be. A well-executed ProfessionaliBranding strategy puts you in the driver's seat and gives you the opportunity to select what you want from the employers that come knocking on your door. I am not saying that just creating a ProfessionaliBrand without "any meat on the bone" will work like magic; you need to walk the walk. In other words, someone who is 100 years old today may find it a wee bit difficult to get accepted into the astronaut program at NASA for the manned spaced mission to Mars scheduled for 40 years from now, regardless of the ProfessionaliBrand she creates. Again, getting the job you want is about taking your wishes, turning them into dreams, and then creating SMART goals to achieve your dream(s) and making sure to follow through with developing your competence.

Some view attaining Level 2 ProfessionaliBranding as a lot of work, and I admit that creating your irresistible offer is not done in one day. This is not a get-hired-fast technique, although it is about getting on the fast track—the GetHiredFastTrack—and in many circumstances does lead to quick job offers. Consider that going to a job you don't like every day, working for an employer you don't like, promoting a cause you don't like, and being underpaid and underappreciated all for the sake of eating and paying bills so you can do it all over again the next day, sounds like a lot of work to me. Writing a resume and doing all that traditional job search "clicking and sending," and begging for a new chance to be rejected in another interview for a similar job sounds like a lot of work to me.

So what do you prefer to do: do all the work to do something that kills you, or do the work and get something that nurtures you and makes you happy? It takes the same amount of work to get a job you are unhappy with as it does to protect your income and get a job that makes you happy and healthy; in other words, it takes as much effort to be miserable as it does to be happy.

BE A PROACTIVE JOB-SEEKER

Once you begin ProfessionaliBranding you are no longer a passive job-seeker or an active job-seeker, but rather a *proactive* job-seeker, and this strategy has many advantages even if you are currently employed. When you are gainfully employed you are viewed by employers and hiring managers as a more valuable commodity because there is social proof that another employer finds you valuable. Human nature is such that scarcity breeds wanting. It is always better to consider a new job while you're employed rather than when you're unemployed, because unemployed individuals are less desirable, as this quote from Mike Rickheim of Newell Rubbermaid from the book *Web 2.0 Job Finder* clearly points out: "The best candidate in a hiring manager's eyes is the one who doesn't have to make a move. They are and have been gainfully employed and there is another employer who really wants to keep them...."[12]

Although you cannot always predict what is going to happen with respect to your employment status, you can control and manage your career by promoting yourself to employers 24/7 with the implementation of a sound ProfessionaliBranding strategy.

LINKEDIN BEST PRACTICES

Your LinkedIn profile is your next step in building your Professionali-Brand.

> LinkedIn is to business networking what Google is to Internet search. If your profile is not on LinkedIn, then you do not exist as a professional.

LinkedIn is the most powerful site for promoting yourself at the professional level as well as the most important networking conduit on the Internet for professionals at the time of writing. Facebook is fast becoming a powerful business networking tool as well, and applications such as BranchOut, and BeKnown are adding a business and professional networking component to Facebook.

LinkedIn is the favorite sourcing tool for passive candidates for most Fortune 500 employers. (Notice I used the words *passive candidates*, not *proactive;* many LinkedIn members are indeed passive and not proactive candidates, because most profiles on LinkedIn have not been optimized, nor are they 100-percent complete, making it difficult for employers to find their profile and be interested in them if they do find them.) It is also the favorite haunt for recruiters. If you're open to considering job offers, are proactive about career advancement, or are unemployed and an active job-seeker, LinkedIn must be part of your job search and promotion strategy.

A Winning LinkedIn Profile

Setting up your winning profile is easy on LinkedIn as long as you follow a few guidelines. Use your SCA and the resume you created previously as a source of information. Start by making sure that you have a *professional-looking picture.* Make sure your profile is keyword-rich for your industry and your professional specialty. (See Chapter 6 for how to select keywords.) Being found on LinkedIn is about search. Keyword density is the major search criterion used by LinkedIn.

People online do not like to read large amounts of text in one paragraph but rather prefer tight sound bites they can scan quickly and determine if this information is for them or not. Chunking information in sound bites or in short paragraphs with statements rather than sentences, using the same strategy as a resume, is a good practice for LinkedIn. Forget about the "I have experience with" statements and use action verbs in your LinkedIn profile just as you did in your resume.

Last name and high Google search ranking

Edit your last name field by adding keywords after your last name (for example: Hill | Job Search Expert).

Professional title and headline

Many people waste this valuable real estate with confusing titles that are not keyword-specific. As mentioned previously many use Google to search for LinkedIn profiles. When an HR specialist or recruiter searches for a manufacturing engineer automotive, the keywords they enter into the Google search bar or the LinkedIn search bar are not "experienced and competent manufacturing guru in the automotive industry." A title like that does not help your chances of being found. Too many profiles have titles that hurt the member's ability to be found. Think about what keywords represent you, and think from the recruiter's standpoint: What keywords would he use to find someone with your skill set? Use titles that are universally accepted; for instance, if your job title is "head honcho of manufacturing," change it to "director of manufacturing." Otherwise you limit your opportunity to be recruited.

Make sure that your LinkedIn Professional Headline is keyword-rich. This will help you show up in searches.

Customize your public profile URL

Instead of just leaving it as the default setting (your name, followed by a bunch of numbers; *www.linkedin/in/yourname/123456789*), make it keyword-rich (for example, *www.linkedin/in/manufacturingmanager*). This helps your LinkedIn profile to show up in search engines like Google.

Set your privacy controls

In order to rank high in search results from search engines (Google, Yahoo), under Privacy Settings make sure to edit your public profile settings and select "Make my public profile visible to everyone" and then select every box except "Basics."

LinkedIn Summary

The summary section is your opportunity to declare your SCA through your profile. It is also important to clearly state why you are on LinkedIn— what do you offer, what are you interested in, and what are you prepared to give, if anything? Here is an example of an excellent LinkedIn Summary created as an example.

Contact me to discuss any help you may require in moving your pharmaceutical, healthcare, and solution provider business forward. We can partner to help achieve your goals by hiring me in a full-time staff position, as a consultant, or as an independent product developer.

Influential and innovative sales, business development, marketing and communications leader, with proven success over 15 years in delivering and selling cutting-edge information and education solutions to the pharmaceutical and health care industries, including eSales and eDetailing campaigns.

Recognized for passion, dedication, and friendly approach in delivering value and in building long-term relationships with clients.

Built robust distribution channels and developed and continue to develop strong network and access to key decision-makers at large pharmaceutical companies.

Conceived innovative first product and built sales from $15,000 at startup in 2004 to $50M in 2010.

First to market with Conversion Plus, RxConversion's proprietary cutting-edge Marketing-Learning and Education Platform destined to be the new standard in eMarketing and eDetailing for Generic pharmaceutical and OTC brands.

Always open to discuss your needs and offer innovative solutions to move your business forward. Contact me to discuss any help you may require or to get introductions to my network.

As you can see, the first part of the Summary is an invitation and call to action—specifically stating why he is on LinkedIn and what he is offering. The meat of the summary is the professional's profile, and the last paragraphs are again invitations to take action as well as to connect to get access to his network.

Current position and previous position

Use a widely recognized title. For example, use "manager" instead of "head honcho." Add as many keywords as possible to your title. There are more than 150 characters; use them. Do the same for past employers. Under experience, "keyword, competencies, backed up by accomplishments" is the best practice to use.

Make sure that your LinkedIn profile is consistent with your ProfessionaliBrand and with any documentation that you send directly to employers. They do check. If you conveniently left out a company that you worked at for only two months on your resume, yet it shows up in your LinkedIn profile, you have a problem.

> **Specialties:** List any specialties. List skills and technical skills. Make it keyword-rich.

> **Skills:** Keyword-rich.

> **Education:** Make sure you fill out the education part because this is a great way to network with other people by finding commonality.

> **Blog:** If you have a blog as part your ProfessionaliBrand strategy make sure to link it to your LinkedIn profile using BlogLink. (Blogging is part of the Level 2 ProfessionaliBrand strategy. See *www.transitiontohired.com/resources* regarding the importance of setting up a blog and on blogging.

> **Resume:** If you attach your resume use a cell phone number and a Web-based e-mail address. Leave off your address.

> **Recommendations:** Get as many as possible. Request them from professionals you know—especially previous bosses. Being found on LinkedIn is about search. Keyword density is the major search criterion so request specific keywords in the recommendation.

Make sure you complete your profile 100 percent.

IRESUMEPRO, SOCIAL SITES PROFILES, AND VISUALCV

The Web has revolutionized the resume forever by improving the ways you can interact in an engaging and captivating manner with your key audience, other professionals, employers, and recruiters. It has also revolutionized how you deliver your message and how many people have access to it. The Web has offered you a virtually free way to have an incredible reach that allows you to bring your message to millions of people frequently, and most importantly to the people who can assist you in getting you the job you want (the decision-makers and hiring managers of the world), plus the referrals of other professionals. If you do not take advantage of this broad reach, in an environment where you now know without a doubt that any person's job and hard-earned pension or employment-based savings can be wiped out in a second, then you are missing out on protecting your income, your security, and, in some cases, your family's security. Make no mistake: The work model is shifting, and shifting fast. It is a stark reality that employees are now bidding for shifts and in some cases employees are also bidding for "shifts and wages." It is just a matter of time before this work model is embraced by more companies. The Elance. coms and the guru.coms of the world have been demonstrating for quite a while now that labor is cheap and people are prepared to fight for work, no matter where the work is located and no matter where the work is coming from or no matter where the worker is physically located in the world. This is not just a Third World or Developing World worker phenomenon; it is happening in North America as well. Case in point: Airport employees in North America are starting to bid for their work, as Kenneth Kidd reported in the *Toronto Star*. In the article "Now on the Auction Block: WORK," he describes the following: "The crux of a labour dispute that has slowed security clearance at Pearson International Airport is a scheduling system that's become widespread in the United States, and whose chief attraction is often cost-cutting. "Dubbed 'shift bidding,' it's a system in which work is essentially auctioned off, turning employees into bidders."[13] As this new reality starts to spread and downward pressure is exerted on wages, because of globalization and the easy access to work from anywhere in the world, professionals will need to be able to point to their strong ProfessionaliBrand in order to justify their bids and guarantee their expected wages. In other words, even though you are a full-time employee, in some cases you are being treated just like a contractor or a consultant, having to bid for a shift and also bid for your wages. Yes, you can resist or even complain and fight it, or you can embrace the big shift in the digital economy that has lowered the barrier to entry—jump on board now or perish.

If you are not being proactive about your job search, great job offers and career opportunities are passing you by every day. Because more and more employers are stacking their HR teams with social recruiters and Internet search experts (just enter the words *social* and *recruiter* in Indeed.com and see how many job results surface), you need to make sure you are found by getting your resume online in various engaging forms.

Getting Your Resume Online

How do you get your resume online? You can post it on a job board site, you can attach it to your LinkedIn profile, you can create a VisualCV at VisualCV.com, you can create your own iResumePro, or you can search with Google and find mobile applications for your smart phone like Pocket Resume.

The Online Resume

It is time to make your iResumePro your best salesperson. Why spend all your energy and time actively looking for work just to be rejected? Just sit back, relax, and have your iResumePro working for you proactively 24/7, bringing you more job offers and career opportunities.

Use your iResumePro as another great tool to put you squarely in your career driver's seat rather than chasing dubious opportunities through "clicking and sending."

You create your iResumePro from the competency-based resume you developed earlier. It is a clear portrayal of your Sustainable Competitive Advantage, backed up with proof of your competencies through your accomplishments. This is not about putting up a bunch of fluff marketing stuff or keywords you cannot back up, like so many so-called experts espouse, but rather making sure you market the real goods on you. It is about establishing your professional credibility. Watch out for these so-called personal brand experts who know nothing about job search and can lead you down the wrong path.

What is a professional iResumePro? It is an independently hosted online media-rich resume Website that highlights who you are and what you do. You own the Website, and most importantly you also own the domain name. This gives you total control over how you customize the presentation of the highlights of your resume. Your iResumePro needs to clearly demonstrate your

SCA. You can add video, audio, slide shows, or presentations. The features you should add to your iResumePro include a PDF file of your full resume for download, a head shot photo, and of course incorporation of a video resume or iVideoResumePro, plus any creative presentations, examples of your work, images, paintings, graphs, charts, awards—you name it. The sky is the limit, because you own it and you also own the domain name.

There are advantages to following through with a LinkedIn profile, a Facebook profile, a VisualCV, and of course an iResumePro and a video resume (iVideoResumePro). Many professionals stop at creating their LinkedIn profile. Stopping at creating a LinkedIn profile is a big mistake because so many free options are available to improve your ProfessionaliBrand, and therefore increase your Internet footprint and attract more job offers.

Creating your LinkedIn profile as well as uploading your resume to LinkedIn is a great start to developing your ProfessionaliBrand. However, it is not the same as creating your own iResumePro with your own domain name. Go to *www.transitiontohired.com* to find out more about the best practices in creating your iResumePro.

I always like technology and other user-friendly Websites that help us build our footprint and ProfessionaliBrand and propagate it for free. The VisualCV is one of these great tools.

VisualCV

Examining online media resumes without looking at VisualCV.com, a leading free site for developing an online resume, would be incomplete. The site offers some really neat tools, and some great resumes can be created, complete with an iVideoResumePro (video resume), audio, images, charts, graphs, and creative samples of your work. A feature available to VisualCV users is the easy-to-use button generator, which creates a hyperlink to your VisualCV that you can then include in all your e-mail signatures. It also eliminates the need to send an e-mail attachment of your resume. You can incorporate your picture into the button as well.

Advantages of iResumePro vs. LinkedIn vs. VisualCV

I am often asked this question: Should I use a VisualCV, LinkedIn, or an iResumePro? The answer is you should use all three. Once you have completed your competency-based resume and your LinkedIn profile, it is easy for you to customize the profile to create your iResumePro and your VisualCV. You can easily import your LinkedIn profile into VisualCV to get yourself started.

Many professionals faced with putting together their online resume believe that a LinkedIn profile is a resume Website, that posting their resume to LinkedIn or to a job board or using a Website like VisualCV is the same as your privately owned iResumePro with your own domain name. It is not the same. It is not a separate domain name, but rather a subdomain within a domain name. Job search is about Internet search, and search is all about keywords and Search Engine Optimization (SEO). Having your own keyword-rich domain name is a search ranking best practice.

Search Ranking Best Practices

Smart Search through ProfessionaliBranding is also about attracting or driving traffic, employers and recruiters to your message, be it your LinkedIn profile, iResumePro, your VisualCV, or your iVideoResumePro, and ranking higher in search results than your competition, thereby significantly stacking the deck in your favor. In order for your irresistibility to bear fruit, you need to be found by an employer, recruiter, or decision-maker.

Ranking on the first page of Google or any search engine and ranking in the top three spots for organic keywords (keywords search results you do not pay for) has some great advantages because most searchers rely on the results in the top three spots to click on, as indicated by research from Optify.[14]

A great advantage to having your own domain name and online iResumePro is ranking higher in search engine rankings. The best practice is to pick a keyword-rich domain and SEO your iResumePro. When you SEO properly you will outrank your competitors.

The greatest disadvantage to only relying on LinkedIn and VisualCV, if you want to promote yourself, is you need to rely on mostly driving traffic to your LinkedIn profile or VisualCV—and by default driving traffic to your competitors who are listed right beside you. You are even further behind the eight ball if you are late claiming your keyword real estate and keyword-rich public URLs on LinkedIn and VisualCV, or even claiming your Facebook page name(s), for that matter. If this is the case, you will need to mount a battle to claim your Google real estate and increase your ranking.

The Fallacy of Googling Your Name to Determine Your Ranking, and Best Practices to Associate Your Name With the Right Message

There are two considerations when it comes to your name. Does the search party sent out to fill a job "not have your name" or "have your name"? The only time someone is searching by name is when they have your name. Remember that most employers that are searching, or *sourcing*, as we call it in the HR and recruiting business, for candidates to approach do not know your name. Some so-called experts will tell you to Google your name to see where you rank, implying that your name alone is what employers search for in order to target candidates. This is nonsense, because I have still yet to see your surname and given names show up in any job descriptions under competencies required! If your name is not Lady Gaga or Justin Beiber or Oprah, no one is searching for you by name. Rather they are searching keywords, representative of the profession or specialty, and usually with a keyword that would focus the search results on location. If they are seeking a pharmaceutical marketing specialist with edetailing experience, they will Google the keywords "Pharmaceutical Marketing eDetailing Boston" or "Pharmaceutical Marketing eDetailing Boston LinkedIn," or search the same keywords within LinkedIn.

Having made the previous statement, it *is* a good idea to Google your name for two reasons: to check for "Internet nasties" as well as determine how well your name, your picture, and your keywords all tie together. Internet nasties are things that hurt your professional image (see Chapter 6 to see where you are showing up throughout the Web and then take the appropriate action to clean up non-flattering results). The idea is to remove the bad stuff and associate the good stuff (ProfessionaliBrand) with you, your name, and your picture. If someone else has the same name as you in your profession, and there are many unflattering results that show in Google for this other person, associate your picture, your keywords, your job title (specialty), and your work history with *your* name in order to clearly differentiate results attributed to *your* name from this other negative interloper. If you have Internet nasties about yourself and you cannot have them removed, overpower the bad with a lot of good results by being aggressive about adding good keyword-rich content associated with *your* name and picture. In other words, be diligent about your ProfessionaliBranding.

So it is not about ranking high for your name, but rather what is associated with your name. You are found based on the keywords and other SEO you use as well as the links that point back to you. Once people have your name and some extra identifying information, such as your company name or past work history, they can find information about you specifically and identify *you*, so when someone is Googling your name it is more about making sure the results represent a great image of *you* and about protecting your reputation.

There are ways to optimize your LinkedIn profile and VisualCV, by having the right keyword-rich headline and keywords throughout your LinkedIn profile and VisualCV, and this is effective to a point. Your own iResumePro presents you with the opportunity to *attract* employers and recruiters to you through simple organic search—that is, by applying SEO strategies to your online resume site to get high Google ranking and get lots of eyeballs exclusively on you through your site. Why is this so important? Because often your name will be mentioned to a decision-maker or someone may find your LinkedIn profile, and invariably, after finding your LinkedIn profile, that person will Google your name plus some identifying keyword. You want positive information that bolsters a strong professional image to show up tied to your name. First impressions are everything[15], so you want a professionally designed iResumePro to pop up so you can control the first impression.

> When you attract employers and decision-makers to your own website you have their full attention—no extra candidates to look at, advertisements to distract them, or other things competing for their attention (like on LinkedIn, VisualCV, or Facebook). You are in control. You control the interaction and experience the employer has, because you own the Website.

If you choose not to create an iResumePro, you do not have a choice but to drive employers to your LinkedIn profile and your VisualCV, and by default into your competitors' arms.

Name and Job Title in URLs and Domain Names

Do not be misled by the claims that LinkedIn and VisualCV are providing you with a unique URL. Yes, it is a unique URL—but it is not the same as having your own domain name. You only get a subdomain of the main domain. It is still the main site's domain name/your name. For instance, the default URL setting on LinkedIn is www.linkedin.com/in/YourName, and the same is true for VisualCV.

For instance, if you are a manufacturing engineer in Boston, for SEO purposes, it is preferred to own your own Website with your own keyword-rich domain, such as *www.manaufacturingengineerboston.com.* A recognized best practice for SEO purposes is to have a keyword-rich domain name.

Benefits of the iResumePro

The clear conclusion is having your own iResumePro has so many advantages. An online resume or an iResumePro is a Web-based resume that acts as a magnet in drawing employers and recruiters. It is your own Website with your own domain name; you control everything. The iResumePro engages and entices employers to interact with you, get to know you, and trust you, and leads to eventual job offers. The versatility and customization options of an iResumePro have totally changed the job search game to a truly proactive game. The iResumePro offers you so many options, including:

➤ Adding an iVideoResumePro, audio, images, charts, graphs, and creative samples of your work.

➤ You can promote yourself by adding a link or button to all your e-mails and social media pages or profiles (LinkedIn profile, Facebook page, and Twitter bio).

➤ Add a QR code to your iResumePro to make your resume mobile-friendly and easy to transfer to another smart phone.

➤ Control access to your on-line resume for reasons of privacy or, if you want to keep a low profile for whatever reason, simply add an access password. Only share the password with the individuals whom you choose to have access to your iResumePro or on-line resume.

➤ Register and own your own keyword-rich domain name.

➤ Take advantage of owning your Website, in case LinkedIn or VisualCV changes its cost structure and starts charging fees you are not prepared to pay. That way, you are not held hostage; it's your site and you can control all aspects of it, including the technology you use.

➤ Control the addition of the latest new technologies and plug-ins as they become available. These are not always adopted by the free social sites.

➤ Put on your Website as much data as you need to support your ProfessionaliBrand, including video(s). Usually, limitations on free social sites or free hosting sites for resumes exist on the amount of data you can upload and have available to promote your ProfessionaliBrand.

- Track who and how many people view your site by adding free analytics, analyze what keeps their attention and what they are not interested in, and adjust accordingly.
- Be proactive in your job search, not reactive.
- Be visible, findable, and stand out as one of the distinguished professionals in your profession who "gets it."
- Gain a huge marketing advantage over your competition that is not prepared to invest in a personal Website.
- Include it in your offline strategy and get greater exposure by adding a link to your BusinessCardResume.
- Use it in some interesting and new innovative job search marketing strategies that make the old ways of doing job search new again. (See Chapter 9 for more information on this.)
- Add a video resume to your online resume to save you and the employer time and money by providing a more complete picture of who you are, not just what you do.
- Update everyone about your new information by simply updating your online resume.
- Prevent going afoul of a non-solicitation agreement if the non-solicitation agreement prevents you from approaching clients from your previous place of employment. By updating your online resume in this way, an old client can easily find you on the Internet and approach you.
- Add your social media icons to your Website so other professionals can easily join your network, share your information, promote you, and easily friend you or invite you.
- Index your site with the search engines to gain more search engine visibility.
- Upload recommendations, endorsements, awards, and certificates.
- Add slide shows and presentations.
- Include a link to your YouTube channel.

In conclusion, the iResumePro or your own Website resume allows you to professionally brand yourself and tie your identity to your picture, keywords, and unique e-mail address so you are not misidentified or confused with someone who has your same name.

Getting the best domain name for the best price is easy. Just go to *www.transitiontohired.com/resources* to find a discount on domain name purchases and Web hosting for your online resume.

VIDEO RESUME

Why use an iVideoResumePro? The iVideoResumePro is as close to a representation of *you* as you can get without actually being physically present. The employer gets a good sense of your presentation skills, your communication ability, and your personality, and a general gut feeling about you. The hiring process is about chemistry, and hiring managers want to hire somebody they feel comfortable with and they like. By selling the employer on *you* with a video before they actually meet you, the employer feels much more comfortable, and that goes a long way toward getting you the job.

Why do you need an iVideoResumePro in addition to or in combination with your iResumePro? The best practice on the Web today is "show it, don't write it"—in other words, use pictures and audio rather than text, because they are more engaging.

Your iResumePro provides tons of good branding information and SEO, but it is not enough if you truly want to be irresistible. Your video resume delivers an even more engaging and powerful message than just reading your text resume alone, be it online or offline, leading to more interest and ultimately more job offers. It gives you the ability to bring your resume to life; an employer can see who you are and not just what you do.

Video resumes, although not as popular as the standard written resume, are gaining momentum and will continue to gain momentum. The reason one develops an iVideoResumePro is to attract employers and recruiters and entice them to find out more about you. The biggest bonus of the iVideoResumePro when it is tagged properly with your keywords is the fact that video presents you with the opportunity to leap-frog your competition in Google search rankings. You can use a service like TubeMogul to propagate your video. (To learn how to use TubeMogul to do this, go to *www.transitiontohired.com/resources.*)

The message your iVideoResumePro needs to deliver is the same message that your resume needs to deliver. The employer must get answers to these questions: What results will you produce for me; what transformation to my company, department, or customers (internal and external) can I expect; and why are you qualified to deliver these transformations and results? (To find out more about the best practices and a step-by-step approach to creating an iVideoResumePro that will make you irresistible, go to *www.transitiontohired.com/resources.*)

SOCIAL MEDIA

Now that your message is ready and you have built your foundation through your LinkedIn profile, VisualCV, iResumePro, and video resume, it is time to "get known" by sharing information. You need to put in place a social media strategy that will expand your network and keep you in the headlights of the people that are important to your career—and, more importantly, get these professionals to like you. In other words, it is time to promote your ProfessionaliBrand and bring your "professional you" to a wider audience. The new networking is all about the virtual connection. Large employers have taken notice and are now engaging potential candidates interactively through social media as well as recruiting and forming opinions about these potential candidates based on their footprint and/or ProfessionaliBrand. The likes of MeshHire are taking hold and making the task for employers much easier than in the past.

The whole strategy behind developing your ProfessionaliBrand in our context is to make sure you are always in the sights of other professionals, so they can get to know about you, get to know you, and get to trust you, lead you to employment, offer you jobs, or employ you. This is why it is critical to have a social media strategy and a focus so you can target your audience and get your message out.

YOUR SOCIAL MEDIA MOTTO

Relationship vs. Transaction-Type

Being a relationship professional rather than a transaction-type professional has its benefits in social media. Consider when creating your social media motto that the social sphere is not about shouting or talking to your audience in the typical "old school" marketing model but rather about sharing valuable information with your audience and/or engaging your audience in a conversation so they take notice and check you out.

Transaction-type professionals have an agenda and a purpose to their interactions. They exchange or network with you when they have a need. They are usually concerned with "What's in it for me?" Relationship professionals, on the other hand, see the value of having a large number of connections, and their message is largely geared to "What's in it for them (their connections and their audience)?" The transaction-type professional seeks an immediate reward from the transaction, whereas a relationship person looks to help and trusts that eventually what goes around comes around or simply gets a kick out of helping others. A relationship professional looks to make many helpful deposits into the "universe bank," whereas the transaction-type professional measures each interaction based on how they can and how quickly they can effect a withdrawal. In other words, the relationship professional is concerned with *affecting* and the transaction-type professional is concerned with *effecting*. Of course each type has its benefits. Understanding this concept goes a long way when creating your social media motto. Will you be or are you a relationship or a transaction-type professional?

Sharing vs. Promotion

The old rules of marketing (shouting and screaming the loudest) do not work anymore in the social Internet world. It is not good enough to tell people how good you are; rather, what holds the most clout is social proof. In other words, you scream your credibility on your profiles and Websites, but not through social networking directly. Rather you leave directions to your professional image foundation by leaving calling cards—links and buttons that direct professionals to your credibility. In the words of Dan Zarrella, in his book *Zarrella's Hierarchy of Contagiousness: The Science, Design, and Engineering of Contagious Ideas,* "Identify yourself authoritatively" and "Tell people why they should listen to you."[16] In other words, let people know your qualifications. If you are an expert or guru, or have accomplishments and competencies, have the confidence to let the world know through your online profiles. Zarella says to think of social media as a networking event. The more credibility someone has, the more likely you are to take real notice rather than pretending to be interested. He says, "Sure, it can be fun to bounce around and talk to random new people, ignorant of who they are and what they do. But the more I know about your qualifications, the more likely I am to actually listen to you, rather than politely pretend." So make sure to create those social media profiles to 100-percent completion, and do not be shy about disclosing your qualifications—this is where you shout—on your profile or bio.

The best way to garner attention is to have raving fans, customers, or clients promote your ProfessionaliBrand. As pointed out earlier, the collective opinions others have of you holds more weight than the opinion you are trying to promote on your own. This is social proof in action. Most social sites offer the opportunity for people in your network to post to your page, to become a fan, or to provide a recommendation, endorsement, or testimonial. You can always ask people to provide their honest opinion.

Social proof for your ProfessionaliBrand comes from professionals telling other professionals how good you are, through endorsements on LinkedIn, liking your page, comments, and posts on Facebook, or even giving you a good score at Klout.com, re-Tweeting your Tweets, or +1-ing (plus-one-ing) search results in Google that they like. Social signals and the capture of these signals is becoming much more prevalent today, and according to some social media experts is becoming a greater factor in Google rankings. Traditional branding is about promotion and association, and social media is about sharing and association. In the social media "sharing" world, it is about being recognized by others for sharing valuable, insightful, inflammatory (which often creates engagement), or entertaining content. The key to creating an effective social media presence is share, not promote, yourself in the traditional marketing sense. Promotion comes from others who endorse you based on what you add to the online stew. The value of your ProfessionaliBrand will rise in direct proportion to how others like you and share or spread that information through social networking. You need to decide what you want to add: choice cuts of beef, shitake mushrooms, turnips, or lemons?

One thing is for sure: Turning up the heat on high right out of the gate rarely works in adding to the on-line social stew; a slow, consistent simmer with just the right spices is the right recipe. Building a social presence takes time, effort, responsiveness, patience, and most notably the addition of sought-after valuable content. As Zarrella points out in his book, "Information that everyone has isn't powerful. Information that is scarce is powerful."[17] In other words, commonplace information is not communicated or does not travel through social media. You want the information you share, tied with your identity associated to your qualifications, to travel through the "social sphere." This is how you garner social proof, get exposure, and attract a following (employers, decision-makers, and the like).

Many professionals get turned on to social networking or start being active in their social network when their backs are up against the wall. If you are seeking quick results from social networking it's too late to put together your social media strategy and start pounding on your connections to create an active relationship when you're out of work. This is not social but rather cold socializing, akin to cold calling. Social networking is about being active in your network, or more importantly proactive all the time. It is about being active in the communities that you are passionate about. This is how you spread your ProfessionaliBrand through social media. It is much better to create professional relationships, and develop and deploy an active ProfessionaliBranding strategy, when you have a job rather than when you are desperate to find work. Having said that, anytime is a great time to start your strategy—seriously, like right now! The bottom line is consistency, and your networking needs to be ongoing. It should not start when you need a job, nor should it end when you find a job; it is a lifelong endeavor.

Social Media: Staying in Touch Made Easy

Previously, keeping in touch with coworkers or other professionals in your industry was difficult to do. With the adoption of social networking you can link with most of your ex-coworkers, coworkers, and colleagues. You can also locate and connect with people you attended school with many years in the past, as well as your long-lost friends. It is important to identify connections in your network that you need to build relationships with. Today that is much easier to do than ever before with all the tools, sites, and applications available for free. With social media you can stay connected to a much wider network.

I believe it is better to create larger, weak networks in most cases than smaller, strong ones. Virginia Postrel, in a *Forbes* article, bolsters my point:

> In an influential 1973 article, "The Strength of Weak Ties," sociologist Mark Granovetter, now a professor at Stanford, demonstrated that while job hunters use social connections to find work, they don't use close friends. Rather, survey respondents said they found jobs through acquaintances—old college friends, former colleagues, people they saw only occasionally or just happened to run into at the right moment. New information, about jobs or anything else, rarely comes from your close friends because they tend to know the same things and people you do.[18]

As I clearly pointed out, the more your information travels to a larger "audience" (your large network), the more chances your information will be consumed by the right person who affects an offer of a new job for you. Build a large network!

Even though technology and the way we interact has changed since 1973, when you distill job search to its purest, it has not changed much since 1973. Job search still boils down to a social component or networking. As noted previously, networking accounts for a large percentage of new jobs landed, and social media is all about networking and building connections. The key, then, to getting the most out of these large networks you will be forming is by classifying them. Use tools like JibberJobber, a CRM, tagging your connections in LinkedIn, or using Google+ circles to organize your networks into communities so you can tap into the right community for the right help when you need it. Strength in networking for a proactive job-seeker is in numbers of connections, as oftentimes there is a clear link by way of introduction from your strong connections to a weak link to the job that is the right fit for you.

Promoting Your ProfessionaliBrand Through Social Media

Being consistent and having "stick-to-it-ness" when it comes to promoting yourself only lasts if you are passionate about the message you are promoting. Otherwise it becomes work and the enthusiasm quickly wanes. This will of course not happen to you, because you have put so much work into discovering your SCA. You do not have to look any further than your SCA to know what the information or content you share should be about. Your SCA has the answers to your passions and what you are good at; promote them and share valuable information about them to attract the right connections! As discussed, the promotion of your SCA—your professional brand *you*—through social media is through sharing, giving, and being recognized by others for adding value. Of course the more you share in different communities on the Web the more opportunities there are for your message to be recognized by others.

Ask the following questions before you post, comment, share, join, like, +1, post on your wall or someone else's wall on Facebook, share your blog with your network, or reach out with an e-mail or a LinkedIn InMail, message through Facebook, or Tweet using Twitter: *Who is my audience? What's in it for them? Is this going to help me achieve my networking goals or hurt my ProfessionaliBrand? Does this add value? Is it scarce information or commonplace information? Are people getting to know me better? Is it a consistent message?*

Delivering a consistent and uniform message about who you are and what you are passionate about in a fun or engaging manner is critical to the development of an engaging professional image.

Your ProfessionaliBrand *message* does not have to be dressed up in a white shirt with a starched collar, a three-piece suit, and a tie; rather, it can be engaging through humor and lighthearted, but it needs to be dressed up to conform with your image. The same social graces apply online as they do offline; being charming works as well online as it does offline. You do not have to limit yourself or confine yourself to creating content, but rather it is the valuable content that you promote or endorse, or associate yourself with, that gets attention. You can post reviews, comment on others' content, repost content, or re-Tweet (RT), and doing any or all of these helps your "cred." Whichever way you decide to add your opinion or thoughts, by creating original content or re-purposing others' content, you can still meet your goal of building a powerful ProfessionaliBrand with those you want to connect with.

The recipe is: Be consistently interactive, responsive, and helpful; update and post; be consistent with your message; add valuable content/information; and always be thinking, "What is in it for them?"

EXPANDING YOUR NETWORK

As stated previously, when it comes to professional networking and making sure that you protect your income for life, it is better to develop a large, weak network than a strong, small network. Deploying an effective social media strategy and building an irresistible offer through proactive job search are about getting your message and your credibility out to as many people as possible, through providing valuable content that generates positive feedback from other professionals in the right communities. By providing high-value information, your information will travel through the social sphere. Your ProfessionaliBrand tied to that information will also travel and get you extensive reach, penetration, and exposure, and expand your network. Having a larger network gives you more chances to touch "insiders," and some studies show that between 20 and 30 percent of all new hires results from internal employee referrals. Obviously the trust factor plays a big role in employers' hiring decisions. Employers trust the opinion of an employee they already know over somebody they don't—another example of social proof in action. So getting insider professionals to know you and trust you so they can refer you to decision-makers is a very important aspect of getting hired through networking. The bigger the network, the more chances of a referral. Remember MeshHire. Can you see how important and critical your ProfessionaliBrand is now? As more reward services become available, like MeshHire, everyone will become a potential "hired gun" recruiter/referrer, and this will cause the 20- to 30-percent figure of all new hires resulting from internal referrals to balloon.

Generally speaking, the approaches in Chapter 8 on networking also apply to job-search networking through social media. Keep in mind other important aspects that need to be considered, such as the following: Follow up on everything and be ready to give. Share funny stories, videos, clips, or pictures. According to recent research, posting with a picture or something like it tends to generate more attention than simple text. Remember: Show it rather than write it. Start expanding your network using Facebook and LinkedIn, and reach out to form new connections by finding something in common. Join LinkedIn groups and add to discussions. Join professional forums hang around in the shadows for a while to get the lay of the land, and then join in. Keep this in mind: "How is what I am sharing boosting my ProfessionaliBrand?"

Hang around in the right communities. Always be on the lookout for groups to join that are popular or specific to your niche, and be an active participant. Look to form connections with people in professional forums and in social site groups. Take the relationships outside the group and connect one-on-one. The best way to establish a strong connection online is through a private message on one of the social sites or through a direct e-mail. If you really want to build a strong one-on-one relationship, provide your phone number to your connection and set up a telephone/Skype video call.

When you meet people offline (that is, in person), befriend them online as well. Many Meetups and networking groups have meetings closely related to your profession or a passion you want to turn into a profession. Meet people in person, grab their business cards, and use the cards' information to reach out to them the next day on the social sites. Send each person an appropriate invite rather than just sticking their business cards in a drawer. Observe the wording of the invites that are sent to you that stir a positive emotion and cause you to take immediate action and engage with the invite. Copy it, save it, and use it if it is appropriate and representative of your ProfessionaliBrand. Why reinvent the wheel? Use what works.

Social Sites and Special Tools to Improve Job Search and Networking

We have already discussed the importance of setting up a LinkedIn profile as the foundation and one of the first online steps to take in your ProfessionaliBranding strategy. Your social media strategy should include setting up a Facebook page with a page title that is keyword-rich, such as "manufacturing engineer Boston"—that means a page or fan page that is different from your profile page. You should also set up a Twitter account that is as keyword-rich as possible. The actual specific content of what you should post and Tweet is beyond the scope of this book; suffice it to say that it should be engaging, interesting, and valuable, and support your ProfessionaliBranding efforts.

Develop a strategy that is an efficient use of your time. Managing a Facebook page tied to your profession and a LinkedIn profile, being active on LinkedIn, responding to groups and inquiries, sending out Tweets, running an active blog, and keeping up on what the Joneses are doing can be overwhelming. Navigating through your network and making sense of your network can also be overwhelming once you start getting up into the 1,000s. That is why adopting some great tools can make that all so much easier. There are many tools available to make your life easier. Social media and social networking sites make networking easy, and as I have clearly shown, networking is a clear winner in job search. All these tools, profiles, and applications, once set up, allow networking to flourish with little comparative effort. Remember to also download all the corresponding mobile apps to your smart phone or mobile device. These mobile apps give you great convenience, access, and the ability to be timely and to act quickly on information, which are great bonuses, especially if you're unemployed.

> The cornerstone of being irresistible is to always be building your networks as well as managing your ProfessionaliBrand using the free tools available for exactly this purpose.

LinkedIn Tools and Apps

Simply sign in to your LinkedIn account and then Google the keyword "LinkedIn" plus the name of the tool or app you are interested in from the following sections in order to download or integrate into your browser. You can go to *www.linkedlabs.com* to see what they are cooking up and what is available for deployment. The following tools and apps are either created by

LinkedIn or by others to exploit LinkedIn's rich features and data. Some features only require that you specify the settings you want.

LinkedIn Signal

This allows you to filter and browse only relevant status updates from your LinkedIn and Twitter streams. You can target updates from colleagues or competitors, and focus or expand your view based on a number of different filters. You can also search for keywords, topics, or people across the stream of network updates, and tap into an automatically updated, real-time stream of filtered content. You can save your real-time searches for quick and easy access.

Some of the neat things you can do are save searches to allow you to check in every day, see a stream of updates from every employee in your company or at a company you are interested in working at, or even keep tabs on competitors or trends in your industry. Also, you can use LinkedIn status updates to promote your brand by providing valuable information, and attract attention to yourself, because all your updates are also propagated through Signal. If you want, updates can be propagated on Twitter at the same time by simply checking the Twitter option.

LinkedIn Toolbars and the options for Outlook , Google Chrome, Explorer, and FireFox

Using these applications allow you to add LinkedIn functionality to your e-mail client as well as your browser, saving time and making interacting with your network easier.

LinkedIn Instant Search

This does exactly what it says: allows you to search your network.

LinkedIn JobsInsider

This is a tool for job-seekers who are interested in job boards and the like. As you know, I am not a fan of job boards, because as clearly stated they are on the decline and offer low probability of success. Nevertheless, this application feature provides information on open job postings at Monster, CareerBuilder, HotJobs, Craigslist, SimplyHired, Dice, or Vault, and most importantly, allows you to see your connections at a given employer when viewing job postings.

LinkedIn Mobile

The application supports iPhone, BlackBerry, Android, and Palm devices.

LinkedIn Sharing Bookmarklet

With LinkedIn's Sharing Bookmarklet, share webpages with your professional network and groups from your browser even when you're not on LinkedIn.

This makes adding valuable content easy. Find an interesting article or content, click on "share on LinkedIn" on your browser toolbar, add a comment or add some insight, and then simply select whom you want to share it with.

LinkedIn e-mail signatures and customized buttons

Create a customized LinkedIn e-mail signature and button. Go to *www.linkedin.com/signatures*. Promote your profile with customized buttons that you can include in your e-mail signatures or on your Website, your iResumePro, or your Facebook page. You can find the link to the button generator in your LinkedIn settings, Public profile, by clicking on a link called "customized buttons."

To find any of these applications, simply do a Google search. Remember that VisualCV also has a great button to which you can attach your picture.

LinkedIn ads

With LinkedIn Ads you can advertise your profile and the job you are seeking to your network. Precisely target your audience. Direct your ads by location, company, company size, title, group, gender, age, seniority, job function, and industry. Your ads can be shown on profile pages, on home pages, in inboxes, in search results, and in groups.

LinkedIn contacts

Export your LinkedIn contacts into a CSV file so you can import them into a CRM or other platform so you can manage your networks.

LinkedIn Resume Builder

LinkedIn says: "Turn your LinkedIn Profile into a beautiful resume in seconds. No more messing around with multiple Word and PDF documents scattered all over the computer. Pick a resume template, customize the content, and print and share the result to your heart's content."

Visualize.Me

This app converts and visually represents your profile. When I first used it, it was a bit confusing, but I soon saw where the holes were in my profile and how I could change the visible *me* to be a better representation of me as a professional. It's worth a look to help you fine-tune your presentation.

Facebook

Facebook gives you the ability to promote your ProfessionaliBrand by creating a fan page that is keyword-relevant and posting to your page wall every day with videos, updates, articles, and links related to your profession. Facebook is the largest network in existence on the Internet at the time of this writing. Facebook is a behemoth and, just like LinkedIn, it can help your professional image or hurt it. Independent applications allowing you to tap into your Facebook tribe for business networking purposes are available.

Google Facebook Friend Exporter

This application for Google Chrome allows you to export your friends from Facebook in order to import them into other networking sites.

BranchOut

This is the LinkedIn network for Facebook. You can use the app to discover new contacts and business opportunities on Facebook. There's a friends-of-friends feature that will help you find connections at specific companies you're interested in, and you can use the app to post and find job openings. On BranchOut you build your empire with your friends from Facebook. All in all, BranchOut is a great tool that will get better as more people adopt it.

BeKnown

This is the professional networking app on Facebook. Now you can connect professionally on Facebook without mixing business and friends. It allows you to connect your Facebook friends for career networking. It is a business networking application run by the huge job board company Monster. At the time of writing, this app had just been unveiled and it may garner traction.

Google+

This social networking site was set up to rival Facebook. One great advantage of Google+ over Facebook is the fact that you can create categories for your networks or circles. Video hangouts were also added. I discussed the importance of getting to know you, versus simply knowing what you do for recruiting purposes, and Google+'s HangOut feature provides access to this "getting to know you" dimension of recruiting in a free and easy way for all parties involved.[19]

HangOut allows you to connect in groups through video. I predict that it won't be long before employers start setting up hiring through HangOuts. It is just a matter of time before employers exploit this feature to cut down on their recruiting efforts to save time and money.

Google+ circles make it easy to separate your network into communities and social circles for professional connections, friends, family, and other custom groups.

As I am writing this, Google+ has just launched and gone live, in a testing phase, four days ago. From what I can tell, it seems like a real winner. I will wait and see and will begin using Google+ once the momentum builds. I believe it is better to concentrate on the proven platforms first, such as Facebook, LinkedIn, and Twitter, and spend the appropriate time there rather than investing too much time in something new and unproven. Case in point: the closing of Google's Buzz.

The Twitter Job Search

What is Twitter? A social networking and microblogging service utilizing instant messaging, SMS, or a Web interface. Sending short messages with limited number of characters. What is the appeal of Twitter? With so much on the Internet vying for everyone's attention, a short message with a link can deliver all you need to know about a subject or whet your appetite for more. Because it is text-based SMS, it is easy to receive messages on mobile communication devices. Here are best practices, applications, and sites you can use to get access to the freshest jobs and content about jobs.

Set up your page to attract employers and recruiters

Make your Twitter presence "employer-friendly."

➥ Put your profile and the job you are seeking in your bio.

➥ Tweet about your profession.

➥ Tweet about your availability.

➥ Tweet to ask for introductions to companies.

Utilize your Twitter background for maximum effect

There's lots of space you can use to promote yourself. Create a Twitter background that is unique and says something like "Hire Me." There are many free templates available on the Internet. Use them.

Include links to your iResumePro, iVideoResumePro, VisualCV, and LinkedIn profile in your Twitter bio.

Twitter best practices

Build your ProfessionaliBrand by Tweeting valuable content. The way to build a following is to get your content to travel or be endorsed. In order to achieve this you need followers. As indicated, if you start Tweeting that you are great, few people will respond. If others Tweet that you are great, many will respond—social proof in action. Do keyword searches of Twitter for the keywords and profession or interest you have. Who shows up and what are they Tweeting? Is it relevant to your space? If yes, follow everyone that adds great content and that has "cred." Monitor Tweets and seek to re-Tweet information you consider valuable. Those you follow and for whom you re-Tweet their information will notice your valuable Tweets and extend you the same courtesy—hence making your message and credibility travel, and in turn generating more followers for you. So the motto is follow, monitor, re-Tweet, and Tweet; you will be re-Tweeted, and your reach will grow.

Job search tools and resources

There are many new Twitter tools and applications to assist with a proactive job search and always more coming on stream—check out TwitJob-Search.com, TweetMyJobs, various job search accounts, and sites like Twellow, Just Tweet It, and TwitterTroll to search out other job resources. Also consider Tweetdeck to facilitate your Twitter management.

Technology and applications are changing so quickly. Go to *www.transitiontohired.com/resources* to find the latest updates on Web tools and applications that will get you hired.

iBLITZ17: DAILY SOCIAL MEDIA INTERACTION MADE EASY

How can you possibly use all these tools and sites to promote yourself? Being active on all these platforms and through all these channels can be overwhelming. Yes, I get it. You're a professional and you are busy; you have a job, family, and personal commitments; you want to enjoy life, not be tied to a computer. First, make sure you get a smart phone and go mobile. You can respond to your audience in real time if you have to as well as monitor and share from virtually anywhere at any time. Download the appropriate apps and see your social experience be transformed, as it has been for me. Everything is going mobile; jump on board or be lost! I resisted for a while but I have found the iPhone with its iOS 5 an incredibly ingenious product and time-saver. Promoting your ProfessionaliBrand can be time-consuming and all-absorbing if you let it, but once your system is set up and interlinked and the right productivity tools are in place with a disciplined schedule and how-to map, you can make it purr along with little effort. If you are not disciplined, social networking can become a life-sucking vortex.

This is why you need a shortcut and a road map based on the latest research that will generate the best return for the time spent. I researched the best data available from Mark Zarrella's book, mentioned earlier, and the data I collected in my practice, and collated it to create "a best of" social networking practices. The iBlitz17 stands for performing an online blitz daily that will average no more than 17 minutes a day over two weeks—some days a bit more than 17 minutes and some days none at all. The iBlitz17 outlines, based on the latest research, the best day and time to post, interact, or Tweet, and which social channel to use (LinkedIn, Facebook, Twitter, e-mail...) on which day of the week to maximize exposure and interaction, and how to incite following. iBlitz17 also outlines how to maximize click-through on any link you might submit through your blog or e-mail, and when the best times are to post to your blog. Why is all this important? Because you want to maximize your return on investment as well as make sure your message travels.

"Drive-Through" Social Networking

Some of you may not want to go to the extent of timing your posts and Tweets, and maybe for your profession you have established your own timetable and want a shortcut. If this is your preference, I recommend the "drive-through method" of updating all your networks in one shot using social managers such as Ping.fm, HootSuite, Buffer, or TweetDeck, on the Web on your PC, or through mobile applications on your smart phone.

The social media god decided to shine down on us by offering us social managers such as Ping.fm. Ping.fm is a simple and free service that lets you update all your social networks at once (most of the social managers mentioned work the same way). No need to go and individually update each one. You will find on the site *www.Ping.fm* the following statement: "Ping.fm allows you to update your social interactions in a snap." Go ahead and create your free Ping.fm account. Once your account is set up, simply link all your social media accounts to Ping.fm. You can enter one post or update, and all your channels will be updated at once, instead of having to go to each individual site and posting/updating your status. I personally prefer HootSuite. Check them out and select one that works for you.

In order not to be continuously distracted throughout the day, set up a distinct Web e-mail address and have all the alerts, Google alerts, feeds, and signals sent to that account. Check this e-mail account once or twice a day, and limit your time spent in each session. If you are a junky and you need your fix, filter your signals so they are manageable and have the most important ones come through to your mobile phone.

PROFESSIONALIBRANDING: THE KEY TO NEVER, EVER HAVING TO LOOK FOR A JOB AGAIN

Regardless of whether you are employed, unemployed, or a student, begin ProfessionaliBranding now. The other great bonus of having a great ProfessionaliBrand is if you decide to open your own business, or begin consulting or contracting, all you have to do is virtually flip a switch and make a few changes on your iResumePro and your profile, and you are in business. By completing a Level 1 and Level 2 ProfessionaliBrand you have your entire Web-based infrastructure as well as your network in place, and this makes it so much easier to transition into a consulting role. Because you did things right you will also have the social proof and the backing of other professionals you need in order to be successful right out of the gate with your new consulting endeavor or your new business. Additionally, you now have true global reach that can attract work opportunities from anywhere in the world, and if your specialty lends itself to it, you can also work remotely from your home base.

> Be irresistible and you will never ever have to look for a job again.

OTHER WAYS TO BE FOUND

For whatever reason if you are still not convinced developing a compelling professional brand on the Internet is the thing to do or it is not your cup of tea, you can still create a positive and professional footprint on the Internet, a mini ProfessionaliBrand. You can also optimize your footprint more fully by using these techniques. This way you still have the potential to be found by recruiters and employers. Remember those Internet crumbs I mentioned earlier?

Other Ways to Get Hired by Maximizing Your Internet Crumbs

Being discovered, or uncovered, by a headhunter or a potential employer is still possible if you have an Internet footprint or optimized Internet crumbs, *and your skills are in great demand.* If your skills are in very high demand, recruiters and employers will leave no rocks unturned in their pursuit. In order to maximize your opportunities, there are some actions you can take to change your crumbs into more of a footprint. We know what happened to the bread crumbs for Hansel and Gretel! As indicated previously, recruiters and employers will do searches by entering job title, company name and/or location through keywords into a search engine of choice, usually Google. In certain circumstances you can help your chances of surfacing on employers' or recruiters' computer screens by using GetHiredFastTrack best practices.

One of the best practices is to make sure your job title, company name, and/or industry and skills, if possible, are publicly available on the Web, through such things as your identification on a business/technical paper, Website for volunteer associations, or a conference attendance list. As clearly stated previously, your name by itself with a telephone number and company does not mean much to a recruiter. It is not your name that is used as a search parameter by a headhunter, but rather your job title, industry or company name, location, and skills that are used as parameters. Your name is really secondary to the search effort.

If you attend conferences, make sure your name shows up in the directories or agendas for the conferences you attend. Volunteer to give informal talks, and/or give formal presentations; again, make sure your name is on the agenda. If there is an opportunity to enter your biography or personal summary, then do so. Many recruiters and employers will troll association and conference sites looking for some trophy fish to catch, especially speakers and presenters. The inference is that social proof is at play: If the professional is good enough to be asked to speak or present, then he or she must have superior skills or knowledge.

Another way is to make sure your job title, company, company telephone number, and e-mail are available in your alumni association information, as well as the professional associations you belong to. Make sure you keep this information up to date. If you move, or change e-mails, telephone numbers, or jobs, make sure to update all your information.

If you are not at a stage in your career where you are in a position to give talks in your professional association, then volunteer at meetings. If possible make sure your information appears in the agenda. If it does not appear, it is still a great step for your career; you will get exposure where it counts and be able to set up a professional network. You may also want to offer your services on an intern basis for an association you are passionate about. Usually your name will be included in the volunteer section of the association's site, newsletters, and conference Websites. For younger workers who want to get a foot in the door, an internship at an employer (even working for free) is one way to go today.

Alternatively, if you are part of a band, a rugby team, or any type of team or association, and can get your contact information (job title and so forth) on these groups' sites, do it. It may sound a little crazy to some, but my team and I have placed many professionals by searching with Google and getting hits from sites for a band, a rugby team, or any type of team or association. The professionals who are tucked away in a laboratory, in a manufacturing plant, or on a software desk are very hard to uncover. These workers are the hardest to find for a recruiter, because their names with accompanying job titles are not prominent on the Web, at least historically speaking. However, that is now changing with sites like LinkedIn (but not everyone is on LinkedIn). Finding a manager or director, contrary to popular belief, is the easiest thing for a recruiter to do. Just call the target company and ask the receptionist, "Who is the manager of contracts?" (Or manager of software, or director of directors—you get the drift!)

If you want to be recruited by a headhunter and placed in a great job, and it does happen, make yourself "findable" to headhunters. A good practice is to alert your professional network that you are open to being referred to headhunters and to headhunter inquiries. If you have a LinkedIn profile and you are unemployed, indicate in your summary that you invite contact from recruiters and you are available to introduce recruiters to your network.

Please note (and this goes for everyone), as also stated previously, if your official job title is something far out there, such as "head honcho of thespians," change it, for online searchable purposes, to something more common, such as theatrical director, or director of theater productions. By doing so, recruiters and others can actually find you.

In this day and age when changes happen so quickly that jobs can be here one day and gone tomorrow, it is imperative, even though you may not want to develop a full-out ProfessionaliBranding, that you exploit the search habits the pros, headhunters, and corporate human resources recruiters use to find talent by optimizing the Internet crumbs you leave on your journey. Take note that these folks rely heavily on LinkedIn-related searches to find candidates, so make sure to at least make the effort to create an effective LinkedIn profile.

Exploiting Your Work Telephone/Voice-Mail System to Be Found

Another approach used by a headhunter's researchers is to troll or surf for names by using a company's automated telephone system. If the company is a mid-sized company, the researchers will call all the extensions after normal work hours and gather all the names. The next day they will work out the job titles by various ingenious methods.

So how do you exploit this researcher's strategy to your benefit? It is simple! Make it easy on the headhunters or their researchers. When you record your name in the telephone system, include your name, job title, department extension, cell phone number, and e-mail address.

Career E-Mail Address

Keep your e-mail address consistent. Ideally you want to provide an e-mail address with a domain name that you actually own—that is, your personal domain name. If you change your e-mail address frequently, recruiters, human resources staff, and other businesspeople will not be able to find you readily. Not only is it important to have a consistent e-mail address that you use exclusively for your Internet footprint and your resumes, but it must also be a professional-sounding e-mail address. If you decide not to buy your own domain name, get one e-mail address and keep it throughout your career. Some examples are Gmail and MSN; although Yahoo is a good service, for some reason I doubt most of my clients want to hire a yahoo on their team. I'm just saying!

Here is an example of how using a consistent Web-based, popular e-mail domain can pay off for you: We had a resume on file of a candidate and it was seven years old. She had worked in the United States for at least 20 years. A perfect position came up that fit her specs. Of course we tried to call her, but to no avail. The reality was, she had moved. We then realized she had a Hotmail e-mail address, so we e-mailed her. It turned out she had moved back to her native homeland, China, to lead the expansion of a new pharmaceutical lab in Shanghai. It also turned out at the time we reached her that her son had just started university in the United States. She wanted to return to the United States and had been seeking a position for the last year with no luck. We landed a position for her two states away from her son's university. She joined as a COO; the company paid for her full relocation and subsidized her housing for six months. She was ecstatic! She got all of this because of a *consistent career e-mail address.*

Make sure you actually put your e-mail address on your resume and on your iResumePro and your profiles. You would not believe how many resumes we get with no contact information on the resume at all. Make sure you keep the e-mail address valid/working, as some Web-based e-mails will shut down your account if it is not used for a length of time.

COMBINING PROFESSIONALiBRANDING WITH OTHER SMART SEARCH STRATEGIES

If you are unemployed you need to find work as soon as possible. You may not have the time to develop a full ProfessionaliBrand and/or you have not left an Internet footprint in order to be discovered by employers. You may need a job quickly, because you have to eat and you do not have the luxury of "evaluating your career options" just yet. This is why you need to get started on your ProfessionaliBrand as soon as possible as well as become a hunter and use the invaluable tools in the following chapters to assist you with networking and direct marketing.

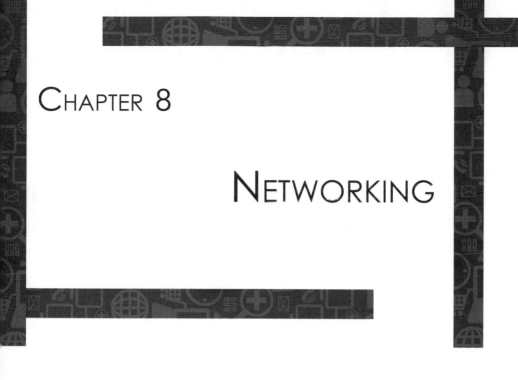

CHAPTER 8

NETWORKING

> "ALONE WE CAN DO SO LITTLE; TOGETHER WE CAN DO SO MUCH."
> —HELEN KELLER[1]

IT'S NOT NETWORKING; IT'S JUST TALKING

When you bring up the word *networking* in job search most people break out into a cold sweat. Most people are not comfortable with networking because they don't understand what networking is. They believe job-search networking is asking people for a job or asking people something that's going to make themselves and the person they are networking with feel uncomfortable. Well, let's put job-search networking to bed once and for all. Job-search networking is not about job search but rather about connecting with people; it is more about being introduced or connecting with people online or offline.

Can you talk? If you can, you are going to be a great networker! If you cannot talk (and some people cannot), but you can communicate through a computer or in some other fashion using your own form of talking, you are also going to be great at job-search networking.

Instead of just calling it job-search networking, let's also call it Job Search Talking, because when you do it the GetHiredFastTrack way that's all it is: connecting through talking. There is no big mystery, and you do not need to read a million books that complicate the whole process by giving it all kinds of fancy words and far-out strategies. Why do we call it job-search networking or Job Search Talking when it should really be called "talking to people results in a job"? Let that image sink in. If for some reason reading the words *job-search networking* brings up bad associations, just substitute those words for *talking to people leads to a job*.

Sometimes a great book comes along, and the book *Highly Effective Networking* by Orville Pierson (Career Press, 2009) is just such a book. Many of the concepts in this chapter and in our coaching have been improved because of Orville's book. I recommend the book as a very good networking resource.

Why complicate something as simple as talking to people you know, who introduce you to people they know, whom you get to know and they get to know you by talking to you or talking to people that share a common interest, and getting to know them through your common interest, be it a person, a news item, a sports team, or profressional organizations, hobbies, children's, or school clubs?

Got that? See, I said it is simple!

How does talking to people result in a job? You open your mouth and speak. Now how complicated is that?

You have heard it so many times: Job-search networking works. It works like most things in life. It takes persistence in following through and dedication to putting in place the best practices you are about to learn. Studies clearly show that talking to people or networking leads to more jobs than "clicking and sending" your resume in response to postings. These studies have been previously quoted in this book. Do we really need studies to understand that getting to know someone through common interests would lead to more hiring than just sending an e-mail or a piece of paper saying "You don't know me but my paper looks better than my buddy's paper, so hire me. I am greater than great"?

People hire people they like, and in order to like them they have to know them, so why not get a jump-start by introducing yourself to a hiring manager/decision-maker before she starts interviewing, or even before she has a job opening. This is part of tapping into the real hidden job market and being proactive by getting inside the mind of the decision-maker.

When it comes to job-search networking, and being irresistible for that matter, it is not the people you know of but rather *the people who know you* that eventually lead you to getting the job you want. Your goal is to take the necessary steps to get yourself known by the right decision-makers. This is just as important if you're employed as it is if you are unemployed. If you are employed it is an obvious proactive approach to making sure you protect your income, because you cannot predict the future. Most professionals have discovered job security is clearly a myth in an era when technology and the financial markets can flip and wipe out economies, livelihoods, and retirement savings in a flash. It is painful realization, as job security is something that is cherished by many yet exists for the very few in the traditional form enjoyed in past generations. Many still yearn for it, but the clear reality is that it is a whole new game that requires new strategies and nimbleness to guarantee one's source of income. The new job search requires you to always be proactive by expanding your network, online and offline, in order to guarantee your income and protect your self-confidence. What does protecting self-confidence have to do with it? As described earlier, invariably most people take a big personal and emotional hit when laid off or fired, so it is best to always be attracting opportunities in order to have a seamless transition from new job to new job.

Many believe job-search networking is not for them because they don't have a network or people they can talk to. It is not about having a huge network. It is about uncovering and using the network you have, and then knowing how to talk to your network. Being a Job Search Talker is also about feeling comfortable and making the person you're networking with feel comfortable during the exchange. It's about respecting one's integrity, values, and comfort zone. You need to adapt your networking style so you feel comfortable and so your approach and techniques are aligned to your values. Of course the rewards you will get will increase as you step out beyond your comfort zone. Let's make one thing very clear: Everyone has a network.

THE GOAL OF JOB-SEARCH NETWORKING

The goal of networking or Job Search Talking is to talk to your existing network through a series of strategic approaches using personal contacts to eventually meet a decision-maker who will hire you for a job you really want. You will learn how to map out your network and then talk to the people in it to easily and productively get a great job. Job-search networking is not simply professional networking; although important, professional networking is just one facet of job-search networking. The purpose of networking is to meet a decision-maker or hiring manager before there is an actual job opening—that is, to tap into the hidden job market by getting inside the mind of the decision-maker. Later, when a job opens up or the decision-maker realizes your skills are a valuable asset to the team, you have the inside track to landing a great job. You will additionally have an advantage if interviews are required, because you will have already established a connection with a powerful ally—the hiring manager—and have tons of insider company information you can use to convince others of your benefit to the team or organization. It just makes the formal interview, salary negotiation, and everything else much easier for both parties, because in this case you're a candidate, not an applicant. This is the distinguishing factor of Smart Search: It puts you in the driver's seat by making you a candidate and not an applicant in every pre-job situation you enter into.

Relax! I promise you it will not be hard to become a candidate through talking to people, and it will be much more fruitful than the old applicant way. You will start slow and easy and condition yourself for more advanced professional networking. Conditioning is a very important aspect. You don't want to jump into job-search networking, go about it all wrong, and have some negative experiences that scar you, and then decide to give up on job-search networking. If you are already feeling apprehensive go back and review Chapter 1, and actually follow through on downloading the recommended meditation. Listen to it every night for six weeks. It will put you at ease and in a better frame of mind.

To put your mind at ease you will begin networking by talking to people you know, and that is easy for everyone. The good thing about starting with people you really know well is that many of you will never have to make the jump to professional networking—that is, contacting other professionals for networking purposes—because you will be introduced to your next job through your close contacts.

This Works for Everyone

Many professionals will want to jump right away to the professional networking section. Don't do it! Follow the process, and you will be surprised how many doors open up for you. I know you are thinking, *I am a software engineer that develops real-time embedded software for internal guidance systems used in smart bomb technology. How is talking to my husband's friend John going to help?* Well, this is how it always ends up working: Your husband's friend John has a brother, Jim, who works at Allied Signal as an office administrator. Jim knows the director of software engineering, Christine. Christine and Jim play on the same company softball team, and they developed a close family friendship. Christine and Jim attend barbecues at each others' houses and their kids have developed friendships, so now they are always in daily "outside of work" contact. It just happens that Jim has been invited to a barbecue at Christine's house and has been asked to bring friends, because they are raising money for the kid's soccer team by selling food and drinks. Of course, you attend as a guest of John and Jim's and you have the opportunity as a software engineer to be introduced to your next boss, Christine, the director of software engineering at Allied Signal. How cool is that?

I am not saying this will happen through the first contact you make, but it will happen—if you follow the process. Do not think you are so high and mighty a person that people you consider to have a lesser-ranking job cannot be of help to you.

As clearly stated, finding work through job-search networking or being referred is considered to be the best approach to getting hired, so if it is not part of your job-search strategy it needs to be. The best approach is to use Job Search Talking with all the Smart Search strategies in this book to get hired.

WHAT JOB-SEARCH NETWORKING IS NOT

When most people and experts refer to networking they talk about informational interviewing, in which one sets up a meeting under false pretenses—the networker does not admit that he is doing a job search. The other ploy they teach is to call someone cold and ask for 15 to 20 minutes of her time, under the premise of sharing some information without being specific about the information, the benefit to the contact, and the fact you are involved in a job search. If you get lucky and she says yes to a meeting, you are directed to pounce on the suspecting victim (yes, suspecting—people are not stupid) immediately with your resume. These approaches rarely work. Although sharing information is a key to the GetHiredFastTrack strategy, most importantly, the strategy works because of the relevance of information you have chosen to share and how warm you make your first contact. Warm means that you have done your research and collected information on the person you are about to network with and you know what connects you or what interests you have in common.

The other area people get confused with is cold calling. Many believe cold calling is networking. Cold calling is an approach that can be turned into networking by using the GetHiredFastTrack process whereby you will be calling into the cold zone. If you choose to venture into the cold zone, it will be very effective when done properly through first doing research and uncovering common interest (followed by conducting a warm call based on the results of your research and providing valuable common interest information for the person you are connecting with). Learn more about the cold zone later in this chapter.

It must be clearly stated that job-search networking is not about giving a contact your resume as an introduction. It does involve sharing your resume or your BusinessCardResume (go to *www.businesscardresume.com* to get yours) frequently with the people you talk with, *but not as the introduction* or the main course.

JOB SEARCH NETWORKING IS ABOUT…

It's about exchanging information and connecting through shared interests. It's about talking to people you know so they can introduce you to people you need to meet in a network. Networking is really just talking—nothing more, and nothing less; just simple conversation. It is about making your contacts feel comfortable and not being pushy about getting introductions or names of people. It is about being up-front and telling people you are conducting a job search but also telling people you are not expecting them to know about any job openings or where a job opening may be. This "non-job-opening" distinction is critical to make early in your conversation.

It is also about understanding what a network is: a group of people somehow connected through shared values and/or interests often called a community or a social community online. It is all about uncovering your networks and contacting the people in them. Your networks consist of your personal network, defined by the people you can call who will answer your call, and sub-networks, consisting of contacts in many categories, including professional, service providers, organizations, and hobbies, among others. Your personal network in many cases will have contacts from the professional, business providers, and others categories.

In order to network effectively you need to be yourself. You also need to be able to share a common interest as a basis for developing a conversation. Notice the word *conversation*. That means listening, not just spouting. It bears repeating that your approach needs to be up-front. Let people know exactly what you're up to—that is, you are conducting a job search. At the same time, you need to let them know you are not looking for information on job openings or help from them that directly will lead you to finding a job. **If you fail to do that adequately, often your networking will hit a dead end and be very frustrating.**

Job-search networking involves developing a plan and a strategy based on collecting information about companies and people, meeting people or talking to people on the phone, sometimes connecting with people that work inside companies (insiders) you are targeting, and finally meeting decision-makers or hiring managers. It involves using your offline and online networks (social media, e-mail list, LinkedIn, Facebook, Twitter, Google+ connections) in an effective manner as well as using online tools and strategies to uncover more contacts. It also means creating a great ProfessionaliBrand, because people will Google your name once you have introduced yourself or they have been introduced to you and learn your name.

GETTING PREPARED

What is great about this section on Smart Search is that most of your preparation is already done from the work you did earlier in Chapter 2 and Chapter 5.

In order to be effective in Job Search Talking you need to know what you want, have a clear goal or objective, and know who you are. This is why your SCA and the profile must be completed. These allow you to communicate your credibility clearly and in a compelling, concise, and complete fashion in order for people to be moved, and to support you enthusiastically to their contacts.

You need to convey your profile through a 30-second introduction and follow with a prepared two-minute pitch that clearly points out your competencies and accomplishments. You need to prepare a resume or at least a BusinessCardResume. Keep in mind that, based on the research you do or the information you gather, adjustment or customization of your resume may be required to impress your specific audience. You will need the target list of employers that you have already prepared. All of these items you should now have at your fingertips.

In this chapter you will learn how to develop a networking map, which will consist of your personal network and your sub-networks, which also includes your professional network, and how to step-by-step conduct effective Job Search Talking.

Finally, you will have to feel comfortable about letting everyone—and I mean everyone—know you are conducting a job search. Feeling comfortable about talking openly about your job search is paramount to success in networking. Choose your words carefully when you convey your employment status; words are powerful. If you are without work now avoid telling people you are unemployed. That word has so many negative connotations for many people and makes them feel uncomfortable. Rather, say you are conducting a job search to get the job you really want or "I am taking the opportunity to evaluate my career options." (I love that last one!)

If you feel uncomfortable about this you have all the tools presented to you earlier to review and apply. Brainwave technology works. Use it.

Managing Information and Your Networks

Job-search networking and networking period will assure your livelihood, and it is therefore a good idea to make it a part of your everyday routine. That is why we developed the iBlitz17—17 minutes a day to building your networks through social media. (See Chapter 7.) This will give you the advantages of knowing where to get information and whom to contact when it comes to your next job search, and also protect your income by being proactive about job search and always being in decision-makers' sights. It makes sense to take a lifelong, career-minded approach to networking rather than waiting until you are unemployed and in a panic to find a job. Use the automated, Web-based tools that are available to you for free to always be prepared and to maximize your career options and opportunities.

As a result of effective ProfessionaliBranding, networking online and offline, and Smart Search (see Chapter 9), your contact list will grow very quickly. You will need to manage the information you collect by keeping records of everybody you contact as well as notes from your discussions. It makes sense to automate everything by using a contact management system or even a contact relationship management system (CRM). One of the great ones that's free is JibberJobber.com. Although it's not a true CRM, it does the job. JibberJobber is specifically set up for job search and networking, and you can also import contacts from LinkedIn into JibberJobber. The nice thing about JibberJobber is it can provide you with visual representation of your networks.

Consider that building networks is a must for career stability; plus, at a later date if you decide to go into consulting or open a business you will have everything you need from a contact and networking standpoint at your fingertips. You may want to give serious consideration to classifying your contacts by tagging them or grouping them using the specific social networking site's contact classification system (in other words, professional, friends, decision-makers, and so forth).

The idea is to set up a great system now, because most likely at some point in your career you will want to or need to turn to consulting or contracting to pursue your passion, and having a way to retrieve information and contact names will be a bonus for drumming up business and consulting gigs. You may want to set up a true CRM system. Many commercial as well as free CRM systems are available. Because you have already set up a great ProfessionaliBrand, it's easy for you to then use the foundation you created to promote yourself as a consultant. With just a few quick changes to your Website and your social profiles, you can point out your availability to take on consulting work, and let the world know you are in business. There is not much difference between the online foundation for a consultant/business marketing campaign and the ProfessionaliBranding marketing approach through a proactive job search today. Having a great information and contract retrieval system plus a ProfessionaliBrand is a career best practice today. Implementing both provides you with everything thing you need to find and approach decision-makers now or at a later date, and land work either as an employee or as a consultant.

The major advantage to setting up your own CRM is the protection you get from running your own application, where you are in control of your data and not at the whim of a Web service or any other service that has a free and a premium monthly pay model which might decide to change its model and start charging everyone, or restrict access to your contact information. Even though they may claim they will never do that, if they sell the service or enterprise to another company all bets are off. Institute a CRM system; it will help you tremendously throughout your life and career. It is essential to have a tracking system of some kind to keep notes, schedules, and contact information. Also protect against someone hacking into your account and wiping out all your contacts; it happens. Be a pro networker and a "career-preneur"—that is, think of your career as a business.

A best practice I use in coaching is to use Skype to make all my telephone calls with a call recorder activated. This way I can go back and review the recording and make sure I did not miss anything important from the Internet calls. Most jurisdictions allow recording of calls as long as the other party is informed.

You can also record everything and have it transcribed by a virtual assistant. Check out elance.com to find affordable services or use Google Voice, which has a transcription feature if you are conversing in English. (Go to *www.transitiontohired.com/resources* for more great productivity resources.)

GETTING STARTED WITH CONDITIONING

First you need to start conditioning yourself. Let me give you an example of how easy it is to start conditioning yourself for Job Search Talking. Let's say you have an interest in pizza, and you like to eat pizza from the best pizza restaurants. You are at a party with friends and you want to expand your network. All you have to do is simply state that you really love pizza and ask your group if they know anyone who really likes pizza—someone who eats pizza more than once a week. Then people start talking about people they know who meet your pizza criterion. One of your friends starts talking about his friend Frank and how much Frank loves pizza. You say to your friend, "I would really like to meet Frank. I am looking to expand my list of good pizza restaurants and I would love to exchange notes with Frank. Do you think Frank and I would get along? Could you introduce me to him? Can you give me his number? Would you be willing to call him, or send him an e-mail and tell him I will be calling about his pizza expertise and to exchange notes? Would that be okay?" Of course, it is a conversation. The idea is not to pepper someone with so many questions all at once; you would take a breath to listen to your friend's responses. Yes, it is that easy. This is how simple networking is: Just talk, listen, and ask questions.

Now it is time to condition yourself and practice so you get good at asking questions that ellicit names and get good at making mental notes of the names mentioned. You can use this technique for any subject, so use it now and start practicing. For example, you can ask your friends about any subject: Do you know anyone who knows a lot about golf putters? Anyone who knows about Ferraris? I am thinking of buying one. Anyone who knows a lot about resume writing? Anyone who knows how to raise nice kids? You get the idea. Be genuine and get started now. Jump on the phone and ask a friend or two about a topic you are truly interested in. Get names of contacts, and make sure to follow through and actually meet in person. Your first reaction might be to think this will take a lot of time. Yes, it might, but it is all part of conditioning yourself to meeting new people and conditioning yourself for future success in networking.

Part of your conditioning and practice is to loop back, thank the source of the introduction, and let him or her know how you made out. It is a courtesy and simply a nice thing to do, as people always want to know how things worked out for you. Try it on a number of different subjects and condition yourself for networking success. Once you feel comfortable with this approach, it is time to move on and apply your new Job Search Talking skills.

BUILDING YOUR PERSONAL NETWORK—YOUR PERSONAL MAP

When building your map you want to concentrate on people you know first—that is, people who would actually accept your call and people whom you feel comfortable talking to. Let's say you only know 10 people closely in the world and they each know 10 people. That's 100 people you could potentially get to know without too much of a stretch. Now let's say you know 50 people and they each know 50 people. That is a potential of 2,500 people you can get to know—that is a whole lot of people! Do most people know 50 people they can call? Get the idea of how big your personal network can grow pretty quickly.

Now write your personal network or personal networking map. List all the people you know who will answer a telephone call from you and whom you know will be glad to hear from you. Name this group your personal network. You can, of course, jot them down on a piece of paper or enter them into Jib-berJobber or your CRM system.

I want you to consider, if you have not already done so, the contacts who will accept your call and are friendly to you from other areas of your life: work, past school friends, professional associations, hobbies, sports, your children and their activities, your children's friends (especially if your children are at least teenagers or young adults), and your service providers, such as your dentist, accountant, lawyer, and plumber. As you can see it does not take long to write down a list that seems to keep growing and growing. This is now your personal network, a group of contacts whom you know well enough that they would answer your call.

List of Company Targets

Retrieve your target list of employers from Chapter 5. It is best to have a list of 40. Put together a list that can be printed out and/or e-mailed readily. This is now your target list, which you will share with your networking partners or contacts.

The first part of your job-search networking will be to contact your personal contacts and gather information/intelligence about the employers on your target list. You simply call your closest friends and tell them you are evaluating your career options by using a unique type of networking. It is important to manage the interaction from the start, especially with your friends, because when you tell people that you're unemployed that might make them feel uncomfortable, and the first thing that will come to their mind is how to help you find a job. Remember to tell them you are conducting a job search (or you are evaluating career options) using an innovative approach to networking so you can get a job that matches well with your skills and ambitions and is actually a job you really want, rather than having to settle for a job that you feel compelled to take because it is available. Explain to your contact that you do not want him to help you find a job directly or find any job openings. Tell him you learned from Paul Hill to put together a target list of employers and have your friends look over your list to see if they have any information about the companies, or if they know anyone who would have information about any of the companies on the list. You tell him it is a big list so they probably will know something about or someone related to the company. If he doesn't, that is cool; you can always spend the time catching up. Also as part of the new job search strategy, you want to get his input on possible companies you may not have thought about, plus fill him in on your competencies and accomplishments. Tell him that the premise of the strategy is that everyone, no matter who they are, can have a piece of information that proves very valuable. Ask him if he would be so kind as to review your list when you meet in person, or you can always e-mail it to him and meet over Skype or on the phone if that is more convenient.

You also want to spread the message about your job search and about your profile. You can bring along your profile through your BusinessCardResume, that great networking tool that fits into a shirt pocket. You can also find a mobile app for a mobile resume at *www.transitiontohired.com/resources* that you can use to transfer your resume from one smart phone to another. You can use the app to create, maintain, and e-mail your resume from most smart phones. This way, all your friends and acquaintances will know about the "professional you." You may also want to provide them with a hard copy of your actual resume, but only after you have talked about your list first and pumped them for information.

For instance, if one of your friends is well connected with the decision-maker at the company you want to work for, you would obviously start with that friend. She may or may not want to make an introduction. Do not assume she is not a good friend if she chooses not to make the introduction. Perhaps she likes to keep her work life separate from her personal life. Take it in stride, and never be pushy or hold a grudge; simply respect their judgment and move on.

The bottom line is to talk to as many people in your personal network as you can about your job search. Remember, you are doing job-search networking to get the word out about your job search as well as gather information so you can be more effective. Your objective is to get names of other contacts that can provide you with insider (a person who works or worked for the employer you are interested in) information about the employers on your list, as well as potential leads to the hiring manager. The end goal is being introduced or getting to a decision-maker, however, "easy does it" at this point.

Do not make a call and start off by saying to your personal contact, "I want to find out if you know any insiders that can lead me to the hiring managers at the companies I am interested in working." That kind of approach will lead to a dead end and will not move you closer to your goal.

Start with your closest contacts—even your spouse or children—and get them to review your list. Practice makes you better and builds confidence, so practice on your family members. Embrace the attitude that everyone has valuable information to share. Who knows—maybe your son's schoolteacher's wife is the CEO at one of the companies where you want to work. Unless you ask your son to review your list, you will never know that a great connection is possible and very likely.

Remember to always be positive and thank people for taking the time to look over your information even though you get no leads immediately. As you loop back to update the people that you have networked with on the progress of your search, you will be surprised how much of an active interest many people will take in your search and how the second time around they may have some very good information for you.

Make sure that you do not bad-mouth your previous employer or complain about your current situation and how hard it is to be unemployed. Keep the interactions positive, and do not get dragged into a pity party even with your closest friends. When the focus switches to concern for you and your unemployment, people are not thinking about the information that is important to you. Rather, they are consumed with emotion and turn to offering support rather than really helping you gather the information you need to move forward.

Here is an example of how an actual exchange may go between you and your friend. Let's call him Bill.

> **You:** Bill, it is nice talking to you. I am wondering if you can help me out. I'm implementing this new networking technique of tapping into the hidden job market by contacting employers before they have any openings. The purpose is to let them know in a more personal way that I'd be interested in working there, and then when a job comes along they will think of me.
>
> **Bill:** Is that not what sending a resume is about, with a good cover letter? I have some cover letters from my old job search you can use as a template. It worked for me.
>
> **You:** Yes I'm doing the usual—you know, "click and send," and the cold calling, and the marketing, and the snail mail. I am also doing this real revolutionary thing called ProfessionaliBranding so that I will never, ever have to look for another job again, but that Smart Search strategy of being irresistible takes time. In the meantime I am pursuing the new networking strategy, and this is different. This is about getting in front of the crowd by making sure that the hiring manager knows of me and knows what I am capable of, and therefore will think of me when a job opens up or create a job for me.
>
> **Bill:** So this way you are not really interested in current job openings but in the potential of one opening up. Is that not a bit risky, just waiting around for something to open up?
>
> **You:** Actually, no. It is very proactive. Like I said previously, I am using all the other techniques from this great book including ProfessionaliBranding, which is creating a professional image of myself on the Internet that employers can find and also

doing direct marketing job search strategies, like sending out my resume by e-mail, and using these new Smart Search techniques I am learning from the book. According to many studies most jobs are landed through networking—up to 80 percent. So instead of waiting around for something to happen I am putting myself in control of getting known by as many hiring managers as I can through this ProfessionaliBranding process as well as this offline Smart Search process. The other bonus to this is—as you know, Bill, there is no job security today, and we always have to be in essence proactive about job search and be open to opportunities all the time, and looking at our next career move. One of the parts of this whole Smart Search method of never, ever having to ever look for another job again is to plan out your next career moves. By doing this networking technique I am guaranteeing that many hiring managers will know me, and then moving to my next job will be very easy should I decide to make a career move from the job that I land shortly using this method. Do you understand the principles?

Bill: Whoa! You really know your stuff. That sounds awesome, but it sounds like a lot of work.

You: Bill, making sure my income is protected for the future and ensuring the financial protection of my family is really not too much work, but rather simply an effort put to very good use. Would you agree?

Bill: Well, when you put it that way, it makes so much sense—maybe I should consider this.

You: Yes, you should. Once I get good at it, I will be glad to teach you.

Bill: That's great. But I don't really know any hiring managers that would want to talk to you.

You: That's okay. I decided that I want to continue as a manufacturing engineer because I really like my previous job. I was hoping you can take a look at my target list of companies and when we meet we can discuss the strategy in more detail. Is it okay if I send you my list and call you back on Monday to confirm a time this week to meet, say on Thursday at 7:00 p.m.? I will buy you a beer at Casey's.

Bill: Sure, but I really don't know much about the companies that I think you are going to be sending me.

You: It's a list of 40 and I bet you will have some information that will help me out. Just look it over and see if you know anything about these companies, or if you can think of anyone who might know something about them, or if you know anyone who works at these companies or has worked at these companies in the past. At worst, we will get to catch up over a beer—and that's a great thing.

Not that difficult, is it? When you meet in person, by Skype, or by phone, simply ask your contacts if they have any information about your target list. If they should mention some names, ask, "Do you think you could introduce her to me and/or provide me with her contact information?" You can suggest they call or e-mail the person to let him know you will be calling. If no names are forthcoming, ask, "Do you know anyone that might have any information on these companies?" and also "Do you know anyone whom you think I should meet?" This can open up a whole new area. For instance, with Bill, Bill might say, "I know this engineer. I am not sure what kind of engineer he is, and you guys would like each other. Who knows—maybe he can help you out." The next logical question would be, "How do you know him?" "Through that guy on my baseball team. I can't think what his name is, but come to think of it he is a sales guy that sells something to do with engineering. He could be a great guy to talk to also."

Can you now see the power of "just talking to people" and how networking can evolve very quickly when you ask the right questions?

Of course, when you meet the contacts your friend has set you up with, use the same approach you used for your friend, but now see if you can get more insider information and if possible, get an introduction to the insider. Insiders are professionals or people who work at the employers on your target list or have an intimate knowledge of the employer, perhaps as a result of being a service provider or ex-employee of the employer. If the networking partner is reluctant to make an introduction, simply ask if it is okay if you contact the person and/or if it is okay to mention the networking partner's name.

When meeting with a new networking partner by way of an introduction from your personal network, start by bringing up the name of the person who referred you and talk about him or her a bit in order to establish some common ground. Tell the person what you're doing, what you're looking for in terms of the job, what you're good at, and that you are not there to ask him for any job openings. Tell him you want more information about the companies on your target list and ask if he knows someone who would know something about these companies. Tell him that your contact thought he would be a good person to speak to about this subject.

By job-search networking through your close contacts, you will eventually be led to a hiring manager whom you will be able to meet or speak to on the phone, in many cases preceded by an introduction from your contact. Most job-hunters like to mix it up and use a combination of personal and professional contacts to achieve success through job-search networking.

YOUR SLEEPER NETWORK

Some of you, after networking through your close contacts and following up with the contacts that develop, may want to start exploring the colder zone of your network. This may be contacts who are sleepers—what I call your sleeper network. These are people whom you know from your past but you have not kept up with. They could be from primary school, university, old clubs, or old sports teams you belonged to in the past. The approach here is to contact people and again let them know who you are, that you are conducting a job search, and you are taking advantage of the opportunity to reconnect as well as get some help in your job search. Your sleeper network, like any network, can prove very powerful.

YOUR PROFESSIONAL NETWORK

You may not have to tap into this network in your current job search because all the contacts you will develop through your personal network will lead you to a hiring manager and the job you want. But this is the most powerful network from a career standpoint, and if you are serious about being a networker for life and in addition protecting your income, then this is a network that you need to develop to the best of your capabilities. Using the techniques in this chapter as well as implementing iBlitz17 will guarantee the continuous development of a growing and robust professional network.

When it comes to professional contacts, they come in many different types. Some contacts, as I like to call them, are wizards who will go out of their way to help you, whereas other professionals for whatever reason don't really care to help you out.

Developing and Nurturing Your Wizards

Early in my career as a headhunter, I was trained to ask for a referral during every call I made to a prospect. If the prospect was not appropriate for a position I was recruiting for, I was supposed to ask, "Whom do you know that you can refer for this position?" It became quickly apparent to me that I received very few referrals for the amount of inquiries I made. I deduced that most likely the problem for the referrer is the old question "What's in it for me?" That got me thinking. What if I took some information from the prospects I called, and then got back to them with something that helped them get what they wanted?

I kept a stack of 3x5 cards and wrote the prospects' names complete with relevant notes from my conversations with them on the cards. If I saw an advert, or I ran across a job that would be appropriate for that person, I called him and gave him the information. At a later date, when the opportunity presented itself and I needed a referral from this person's industry, I would call on him for a return favor. What I found was that, by giving first, the positive responses to my requests were much greater, as was the quality of the referrals I received.

For the people who provided me with a referral, the word *wizard* would be marked on their 3x5 cards. I would then separate my wizards by specialty, making it easy for me to find a wizard when I needed a specific referral.

Why the Word *Wizard?*

Wizards are by nature magical because they can make things happen. While my colleagues spent so much time working with poor results, I turned to my wizards and, just like magic, perfect referrals appeared.

The methodology I used to keep my prospects informed was based on noting any leads or jobs that might be appropriate for my database of prospects and calling them with that information.

Through the years, I cultivated a great group of wizards, and we were able to trade much valuable information. This sharing of information is to what I largely attribute my business success as a professional recruiter. If you are employed or unemployed, start now and develop a group of wizards.

> Embrace the GetHiredFastTrack wizard's mantra: "Give and thou shall receive." You never know when you might need your own wizards to make magic for you.

If you are unemployed, be prepared to give valuable information. If you hear of a job that may be good to a fellow job-searcher, be he employed or unemployed, pass it on and ask the person to keep his eyes open for you also.

Remember: Networking without giving back soon dries up the well, and you are quickly viewed as an information-sucking leech. Instead, use and live by the wizard's mantra.

Dealing With Perceived Rejection

Sometimes when contacting people at work or in your professional network, you may catch them when they are busy or preoccupied, and they may seem less than friendly. Just chalk it up to your timing not being optimal. It happens; no big deal. You just got them at a bad time. Do not view a bad exchange as negative and a rejection of you. It is a rejection of your proposal or anticipated proposal; it is just business. React professionally by saying, "Did I catch you at a bad time?" Don't even wait for a response, and say, "Let me call you back," and hang up. I am pretty good at detecting people's moods by their voice inflection, and rather than wait for a "no, it's okay," I have learned that changing people's moods when they are entrenched can be very difficult, because they are focused on the issue that is bothering them or invested in their mood. Rather than following through with my pitch, I just say I will call back, and hang up. A less-than-ideal response should not hold you back from following through the next day. Be persistent. Keep your eye on your goal, visualize the job you want, use your guided meditations, and go for it.

Non-Insiders, Insiders, and Decision-Makers

Your professional network consists of people associated with your profession and who are classified as non-insiders, insiders, and decision-makers. These terms are defined as follows:

Non-insiders are professionals who know your industry or work with contacts in your profession or industry but do not work directly at the targeted employers on your list.

Insiders are professionals who work at the employers on your target list.

Decision-makers are people who make the final decision or highly influence the final hiring decision at the target employers. Decision-makers are the contacts you ultimately want to meet and who will be introduced to you through your non-insider or insider networking partners.

> Talking to the professionals in your professional network will lead to introductions to decision-makers.

There are many benefits of networking with your professional network that can make your whole networking endeavor much easier. You may find an insider who is a cheerleader and promotes you internally to a specific hiring manager or generally through HR. I am not saying this is necessarily the reason for the help from the cheerleader, but a nice bonus for your cheerleaders is that they can often make some money from promoting internally, as many employers offer bounties in the form of cash payments for referrals that result in new hires. The bounties usually start at $2,000 and go up from there. A service called MeshHire, now used by many employers, including Fortune 500 employers, to manage social network recruiting functions, has a reward system built in. The reward is in place to entice current employees to refer potential candidates from their social network and in doing so receive a reward from their employer. This type of service has the potential of turning every employee or professional into a recruiter for bounty—hence even more reason to create a great professional Internet image.

When you do get favorable treatment, and any time you are put in touch with a decision-maker—even if it is just a quick hello—make sure to treat the exchange, no matter how trivial, as though it is a formal interview, because in essence it is. Every exchange with professionals is an interview, especially with decision-makers. This also goes for meeting an insider at the employer's facility for networking purposes. Make sure you dress appropriately and be on your best behavior, because you will be crossing paths with other professionals as well as perhaps being introduced to a decision-maker, and you want to make a solid impression.

> Whenever you are introduced to a group of people that includes a decision-maker, the mistake most job networkers make is to exclusively focus all their attention and questions at the decision-maker. Avoid doing this. This is an opportunity to show your social and teamwork skills, so include everyone in your discussion. Do not turn your back on anyone. The decision-maker will be paying attention and will notice your lack of social skills if you start cutting people out of the discussion and are non-inclusive.

Another great advantage to tapping into your professional network of non-insiders and insiders is their ability to draw you a map of how to get to the decision-maker. Using tools like LinkedIn and JibberJobber as well as a good CRM system can help you map out your path to get to the decision-maker.

GIVE OTHER PROFESSIONALS A COMPELLING REASON TO MEET WITH YOU

Professional networking is about information sharing and sharing profession-specific, high-value information/high-value content that will benefit your professional networking partners. Obviously if you've got some information that's of great interest to people in your profession, they will be interested in speaking with you. You should put some serious effort into researching a specific specialized topic—a niche subject—in your profession or industry and become an expert on it. Make sure it is something that will engender interest and would be appropriate across all or most of the companies on your target list. Usually a topic about best practices in your profession is a good place to start. In addition, other information or content you can share includes information about competitors as well as specific people in the industry, articles, or book summaries. Everyone loves to receive a book summary of professionally important but boring technical information condensed to a 10- to 30-page read.

Beyond having good information to share, do your homework and get comprehensive background information on the professionals with whom you are about to network. Use social media, LinkedIn, Facebook, Google+, and Google, as well as asking the person who referred you for insightful information on your future networking partners. Also make sure you have gathered all the relevant information about the employer you are specifically targeting before the meeting.

You look like a real amateur and embarrass the person who referred you if an insider asks you what you know about his company and why you want to work there and you come up with a blank answer. Do your homework. Shortcuts do not work in Job Search Talking and are even more of a no-no at the professional networking level.

While doing your information topic research, you will come across articles, and in many of these articles experts will be quoted. Use your professional network to see if it intersects with someone who can make the introduction to the expert in the article. Experts are always flattered to be called upon, and you can use the article as a common point of interest. In networking with experts or with other professionals, good opening lines are "I need your professional advice," "What is your professional opinion?" or "Professionally, what do you think...?" These always work to engage the other party.

FEAR-BASED WHITE PAPERS

You may also want to write a white paper or a research paper that you offer to insiders and suggest they pass it on to the decision-maker. You may in addition prepare a presentation and offer to make the presentation for the employer. This way you are able to reach a large group of decision-makers in one shot. You will want to review the details about fear-based marketing, as it is explained in Chapter 9, and then adapt it and use it as a powerful attention-grabber in your networking.

Here is an example of the approach. Let's say you're a manufacturing engineer. You can contact your professional network, and let them know that you've been studying and have written an interesting paper on the latest technology and how it can be used today to cut costs as well as boost production. Specifically you've looked at Robot 3ZX3 and how it can save companies' money in a flexible manufacturing environment because of certain unique properties that would benefit your target list. You can mention to your insider that you have prepared the paper but you have also put together a presentation. The presentation demonstrates the future losses for companies that don't implement the technology now, and you also have, as a bonus, research and insider information that shows how their competition is using it now to gain a big advantage over their competitors. The title of the presentation could be something like "The 5 Things Your Strongest Competitors Are Doing Now With Robot 3ZX3 in Order to Crush Their Competitors and Drive Them out of Business." Which manager or company leader would not want to listen to a presentation that could save his company?

For instance, in my business of job search, I often suggest the following presentation to an insider of a professional group, such as accountants, engineers, and the like: "The 7 Killer Strategies GetHiredFastTrack Job Search Graduates Are Actively Implementing to Make Sure You Don't Get the Best Job Offers and They Do." I invariably get a call back from the contact or one of the group representatives saying, "We are available when you are to speak to our group, since this topic is of great interest to all our members."

Obviously if you're discussing a topic that is relevant to your profession, and you have chosen wisely with respect to the topic relating well to the job you want, the next logical step is to ask the professional contact if she knows anyone who has more information about your particular topic or closely related to your topic. When she mentions a name, ask if it would be appropriate if she set up an introduction, and also ask the standard information-gathering questions: "How do you know this person? What is he like? Do you think we would match up well? What is his background? Just in case you are unable to make the introduction, if you are unable to reach him, is it okay to mention your name if I find him? What is his contact information?"

You may consider going much more in depth about the subject with your insider and offer to share authorship if she contributes to the paper as well as offering to conduct a joint presentation if she agrees to get you an introduction to the decision-maker or a presentation to the department.

How to Approach Professional Contacts by Telephone

Professional contacts are usually busy, and they will want to know who you are, what the call is about, and how they know you. Start by telling them your name, your profession, and where you are formerly from (for example: "My name is Natasha Smart and I am a networking manager who worked formerly with AT&T."). Tell him what kind of information you have and bring up the name of the person who made the introduction as a point of common interest. Follow with explaining that your mutual contact suggested that your target may be interested in the professional information you have available. Lead your target to pick a meeting day and time by asking, "Are you available on X day at X time or Y day at Y time?" to discuss the subject matter.

Hopefully your target will pick up on the use of the words *formerly with AT&T* and ask you about it ("What do you mean by formerly?"), at which point you can tell him about your job search. If he does not ask, make sure to fill him in on your job-search networking approach. The respectful thing to do is ask if he has time to talk. If he is like most professionals who work a tight schedule, he may not be available immediately to talk. Tell him that you can respect that he is busy, and ask him to meet with you over coffee, or on a video call through Skype and you will send him a coffee by e-mail. In my, and my clients' experience, it usually gets a good chuckle. (See the boxed text that follows.) It is best to offer a choice of times rather than asking, "When are you available?" Leaving it open usually leads to, "I will get back to you." Instead, always give a choice (for example: "Are you available on Tuesday at 12 by Skype or Wednesday at 7:00 p.m.?").

Skype eCoffee

One of the things I instituted in my coaching practice is the video Skype and eCoffee networking call as a networking technique. As a networker you can send someone a virtual eGift, which I call sending an eCoffee to the person you hope to connect with.

You can send your networking partner(s) a pre–Skype meeting ecoffee, or in essence an eGiftcard. Go to *www.Transitiontohired.com/resources* for more information.

I suggest you budget 50 eCoffees for your job-search networking campaign. I will bet this will be the best $250 you will ever spend. People like simple gifts as rewards for their efforts. You most likely will quickly recover the cost of investment in time less traveled and in cost of transportation saved.

Many professionals do not want to make the time available because they mistakenly believe you will pump them for information on job openings, they may not want to meet you in their offices, or meet you period, because they really don't know you yet. When faced with this situation, I tell my clients to break the ice by offering an eCoffee and suggest a call over Skype to get to know each other. The friendly gesture of an eCoffee gift always works to warm up the relationship.

During your Skype networking call, use the same approach you used with your personal network. When you get a meeting with a professional contact, make sure you stay alert for any names that are mentioned in the discussion. Write them down and bring them up at the end of the conversation, and of course ask for an introduction. You want as much information as you can get about the introduction so ask something like, "Can you tell me a little bit more about her?" Don't get discouraged if you don't get names of contacts at every meeting. Just getting your message out is great. Eventually your message will find its way to a hiring manager.

Remember to loop back and contact your networking partners more than once. Follow up with them and keep them informed. Every new conversation has the potential to open up the lead that gets you the job you want. It is also a good practice to follow up with a handwritten thank-you card after a meeting.

Ideally at the end of your meeting, the result you are after, with a non-insider or an insider, is to be passed on to the decision-maker. In order to facilitate that process you can state something like, "I know that they're not hiring right now but I'd really like to meet or speak with Mr. Boss, because sooner or later based on attrition they will need somebody. Would you be willing to make an introduction?" In some situations your contact may ask for your resume instead and tell you he will pass it on to the decision-maker. Tell him that is a nice gesture and you appreciate it but remind him that the purpose of the job-search networking is not to find immediate openings (although that would be ideal) but rather to be in the decision-maker's sights when the next opening becomes available. Tell him you would prefer to present it personally and you would really appreciate an introduction. Once you agree to send the resume, the exchange is usually dead. Reserve the resume to be the last item of your exchange. Deflect the request for the resume and carry on with your information-gathering.

To find more professional contacts and connections to decision-makers, consider using LinkedIn and marry it to JibberJobber. Export your LinkedIn contacts and enter them into JibberJobber. By combining the best of both, you have a powerful tool that allows you to map your network and see graphically where your network interconnects, what path to take, and whom you can contact to get an introduction to the decision-maker. New features are always being introduced on LinkedIn and other social sites, so check frequently to find out what is available to make your life easier.

Making connections with decision-makers is the ultimate goal of job-search networking. You ultimately want to get the decision-makers' names and as much information as you can about them. This way when you do get an opportunity to meet a decision-maker, you will be well prepared. You want to get full names, job titles, e-mail addresses, and telephone numbers. Ask questions of your professional networking contact that will elicit valuable information about the decision-maker and also some critical problems or pet projects that the decision-maker may have on the go.

Once you have finished your meeting with your professional contact and in preparation for meeting the decision-maker she has introduced you to, make sure add to your research and see if you can uncover points of common interest between you and the decision-maker (for instance, common universities you attended, hobbies such as golfing, or belonging to the same special associations).

The Web is a powerful tool to be used in this instance for gathering information. Tools like LinkedIn and Facebook can offer so much insight. Often information about the decision-maker can also be gleaned from the news page on the employer's Website.

CONNECTING WITH THE DECISION-MAKER

Before you connect with a decision-maker make sure you have reviewed Chapter 10 extensively; also remember that every contact with a decision-maker is an interview. You never know when it may turn into a classic interview, so always be prepared.

Of course, when connecting with a decision-maker, using a point of common interest, such as an association, hobby, or the person who referred you, is always a great strategy. Of course, as a way of introduction to your conversation, you need to let him know who you are, why you are calling, what's in it for him, and how long it will take. The approach is the same as with any other professional contact. Take the approach that you have some great information and you want to share it by way of job-search networking and by meeting with decision-makers like him. This way, when the time comes and there is a position available in his department or the company that would be suitable, you would like him to think of you and contact you.

After your meeting with the decision-maker, your job is to stay in contact with her by following up and/or providing more information in time. You want to keep in her sights for now and for the future. In order to do so, call her, or send a short update note periodically and let her know you're still interested to be considered if an opportunity comes up or if she has a relevant problem that she needs solved.

CONSULTING AS A JOB SEARCH/NETWORKING STRATEGY

One way to effectively network at the professional level is to offer your services as a professional consultant. The problem is everybody who is unemployed is claiming they are a consultant. Make sure you stand out and you are taken seriously by approaching it as a business. Take being a career-preneur seriously. Use the techniques in ProfessionaliBranding to build your online presence. Build a business Website; set up a business plan, a marketing strategy, a marketing package portfolio, a business address or a virtual business address, and use the networking expertise you have developed here to get in front of decision-makers. You may be hired for a contract and then offered a full-time position, or simply offered a full-time position. A professional business offer is a great way to get in front of decision-makers.

WARMING UP YOUR CALLS INTO THE COLDER ZONE

If you feel the need to expand your network beyond the communities, groups, and networks already mentioned to what I call a colder zone or into colder calling, then please do so. This may be the case if you are seeking a "specialist" position as defined in Chapter 5. The way to approach potential contacts in the colder zone, be they decision-makers or not, is to find some common point of interest. By doing so you are warming up the call. Discovering you went to the same school, or you have similar interests or something in common, is usually the thread that opens up discussion. You can really get into your sleeper network this way or get into some very cold zones by using the information available through social networking on the Internet.

Some people are very good with colder calling, and others are not. Good colder callers are people who can establish a connection quickly. They are able to find common ground with the person with whom they are speaking. All networking is about establishing a connection through talking, and everyone is capable of developing skills in this area.

FACE-TO-FACE, VIDEO CALLS, TELEPHONE, AND E-MAIL

I believe it is always more productive to meet someone in person, and barring that, at least by video. (Make sure to visit *www.transitiontohired.com/resources* for tips on how to conduct a video interview and to learn the ins and outs of making a good impression through a video call or Skype video call.) The next best way to connect is through a telephone call. Barring that, e-mail. To personalize the e-mail, you can always use your voice recorder on your computer and attach an audio file to your e-mail. An audio message is a nice personal touch. When you don't have someone's telephone number, this is a good way to turn the e-mail resources you do have into what is in essence a telephone message. Limit your recordings to one minute.

Computers are great for doing research and for organizing information, but a job search is personal, and you're better off contacting people directly than sending impersonal e-mails. There's nothing wrong with sending an e-mail if that's your last resort. Most importantly, having a conversation, actually connecting with somebody is what job search networking is all about. It has been my experience that attaching an audio recording works where simple text e-mail does not.

WHAT TO DO WHEN YOU GET YOUR NEW JOB

When you do land your new job make sure to let everybody know, especially those with whom you networked. Give them your e-mail address and offer them some help in their job search or help in learning networking.

Once you have your new job, it's important to continue to build your professional network. Continue to offer great information and remember that by giving your best information and leads, you develop your wizards and, consequently, you'll never, ever have to look for another job again. Stay in touch with all the decision-makers, let them know what you're up to, and give them an update every six months. This way you guarantee you're always in their sights, and if something great comes up you can always consider it. Develop an impressive ProfessionaliBrand coupled with an effective iBlitz17 strategy, and you will always have some valuable information to share with your professional network, as well as the decision-makers in your professional network.

The best way to be remembered is to buy a copy of this book, enter a thank-you note on the front cover, and send a copy to those people who helped you in your job search. People are very reluctant to throw out business books or self-help books. This way, they will put the book on a shelf and every time they see it they will think of you. Just go to a site like Amazon and have it shipped to them directly, or go to *www.transitiontohired.com/resources* for great deals on this book.

CHAPTER 9

SMART SEARCH THROUGH DIRECT MARKETING

"THERE ARE RISKS AND COSTS TO ACTION. BUT THEY ARE FAR LESS THAN THE LONG RANGE RISKS OF COMFORTABLE INACTION."

—JOHN F. KENNEDY[1]

Combining an effective ProfessionaliBranding strategy with job-search networking through social media and through talking is a proven method to accelerate job-search success. If you are just starting off building your ProfessionaliBrand it will be a while before you will "Be Irresistible." This is where direct marketing in combination with networking and becoming a job-hunter will pay great dividends. As you now know counting on "clicking and sending" or on headhunters to find you a job is *not* a great strategy. Combining direct marketing with some of the tools and strategies from what you learned about ProfessionaliBranding is an effective, proven way to track down your next job.

DIRECT MARKETING THE GETHIREDFASTTRACK WAY

➜ Direct target marketing

➜ E-mail engagement marketing

➜ Fear-based education marketing

➜ Marketing letters

➜ Free-agent offer convert to contractor or perm

You are the hunter. You take control of your outcomes. You do not sit back and wait; you strategize and take action. Are you thinking, "I am not a hunter?" Okay, that is fine, but sometimes you just have to do what you are not comfortable doing in order to survive. Yes, ideally you want the right job, but you might just have to do with something that pays the bills until you devote more time to ProfessionaliBranding—what I call a survival job. There is no harm or embarrassment in that; just do what you have to do.

> Become a hunter and follow the tracks—the GetHiredFast-Track—to your next job.

You need to focus on the stuff that brings the best success rate in job search, and that is networking and direct marketing. With the innovative strategies you are about to learn, you will be able to substantially increase your odds because you will not be doing traditional cold call marketing (which has a low success rate) but using proven techniques that get you hired. You may feel a slight tinge of fear creep in as you are faced with deploying some of these methods. Go back to the earlier chapters and do a refresher on the use of visualization and positive self-talk as well as meditation to combat the fear.

HOW TO GET THE HIRING MANAGERS' NAMES AT YOUR TARGET COMPANIES

Your target list from Chapter 5 will now be used as a map for targeting hiring managers and decision-makers at the companies of interest. There are a number of different approaches to getting hiring managers' names:

➜ Direct telephone calls to the employer.

➜ Web-based research

     ⇨ LinkedIn searches

     ⇨ Internet search engines such as Google

  - ⇨ Association searches
  - ⇨ Searches of social networking sites like Facebook
  - ⇨ Using Wink People search, a powerful tool that searches all social media (*www.Wink.com*)
- Referrals through networking

Direct Telephone Calls to the Employer

This is the first approach to be used. Make the call to reception, and ask for the name of the person responsible for a particular department. For instance, if your passion is being a maintenance electrician, you would call the switchboard, and ask for the name of the electrical maintenance supervisor or the maintenance manager. This is by far the most efficient, time-wise, to get a hiring manager's name. This sometimes works; sometimes it does not. Sometimes reception operators or gatekeepers are told not to give out names. If that is the case then consider using the following tactic: voicemail surfing.

Getting Around the Gatekeeper Using Voicemail Surfing

Use automated telephone answering system surfing to break through and reach your target. A great article by G. Pankow about voicemail Surfing[2] will show you how to surf various telephone answering systems based on their brand name. In the article the author teaches you how to recognize what brand name system you are up against, and the telephone key strokes you need to use to be most efficient in your surfing. Once you are able to surf proficiently, you can get the contact names you need. Remember: You are surfing for the greater good of the company you are targeting. You believe the company will benefit by hiring you. If you do not believe that is the case, by all means do not surf or call the company under any circumstances.

Web-Based Research

Using Google to search LinkedIn is an effective way to get hiring managers' names, or names of potential referral sources to be used for networking. By using Google rather than LinkedIn directly, you circumvent the need to have extensive LinkedIn connections.

Table 9.1 Plug and Search: Google Search Strings 2

	Keyword	String	Example
Search 6	Contact name search for a Maintenance Supervisor at a specific company in a target city	inurl:LinkedIn.com intitle:LinkedIn "hiring manager title" "location"	inurl:LinkedIn.com intitle:LinkedIn "General Motors" "maintenance Supervisor" "Detroit area"
Search 7	Contact name search for a maintenance supervisor in a target industry and specific target	inurl:LinkedIn.com intitle:LinkedIn "keywords for industry" "location"	inurl:LinkedIn.com intitle:LinkedIn "automotive" "Maintenance Supervisor" "Detroit area"
Search 8	Owner or president names from small industry-specific employer in target location using special keywords and telephone area codes for surrounding city search	"industry keywords" "testimonials" "owner OR President OR Founder OR CEO OR Director" "Area codes for location"	"business cards" "testimonials" "416 OR 905 OR 647" "owner OR President OR Founder OR CEO OR Director"

To get the search strings in a ready-to-go format, simply go to *www.transitiontohired.com* and copy the search strings and paste into Google.

Hiring Managers' Names at a Specific Company

See Search 6 in Table 9.1. For example, let's search for names of maintenance managers/supervisors at a specific company on your target list prepared in Chapter 5: General Motors. The keywords are to be entered in order of importance into the Google search bar, and for Search 6 the keywords would be related to name of employer, then job title, followed by location (in our example, General Motors, Maintenance Supervisor, and Detroit area). It is important to use Boolean operators (AND and OR) and to exactly replicate the search string. See Search 6 in Table 9.1 for an example and the exact search string you can replicate to do a similar search.

Hiring Managers' Names by Industry and Location

See Search 7 in Table 9.1—specific geographical location but with no preference for specific employer. Search keywords related to job title, industry-specific keywords, and location (in this example, Maintenance Supervisor, Automotive, and Detroit area).

If the following line shows up in your results make sure to click on it to get additional results: *"repeat the search with the omitted results included."* This is a very important step, because some searches may show three results until you search again with the omitted results, and the *new unique search results* will balloon into the 100s or even 1,000s.

Hiring Managers' Names From Small Employers in a Preferred Location

See Search 8 in Table 9.1. Let's say you wanted to work in a small printing shop. In this case you will need the name of the owner or manager of the company in order to approach him. You will search with job title, the word Testimonials (because smaller firms have a testimonials page on their Website; large corporations typically do not), and the telephone area codes for the geographical area you are interested in.

Tweak the search strings in these examples for your own needs. Change the keywords as you see fit. Make sure to respect the integrity of the composition of the search string (that is, correct spacing ,- signs, quotes, and so forth). Otherwise, your searches will not be effective. Consider going back to Chapter 5 to review the information on "Google search tips."

Remember also to click on *"repeat the search with the omitted results included."*

REFERRALS THROUGH NETWORKING

Call or talk to someone at the company who can refer you, or pass on the name of the hiring manager you seek. If you know the name of a salesman at a company, call and ask him, for instance, in the previous example, what the name of maintenance manager is. You will be surprised how many times salespeople will help you. Why? Because they make their living on referrals and networking, and are eager to help out, especially if you can return the favor and pass on some information to them.

Asking for Referrals

Expand your network by using the names you have uncovered through your Google/LinkedIn searches to approach professionals and ask for contact referrals. If you are conducting a cold call, you will usually be asked by the person you contact how you got their name, or who referred their name to you. If the referral source has given you the okay to divulge his or her name, then by all means, go ahead and provide your new contact with the source of the referral.

I suggest that you also be preemptive and let the contact know that the referral gave you permission to use his name as the source of the referral. This way the new contact feels comfortable in the event he provides you with a referral that you will also keep his name confidential and only divulge his name if given permission to do so.

Often potential referral sources are afraid to pass on the name of a hiring manager for fear of perceived reprisals from the hiring manager. They will get off the hook by saying something like this to you: "You need to go through human resources." In these cases, assure the person that you will keep the source confidential if that is her wish.

How to Get Contacts to Give You Referrals Even Though They Are Reluctant

Many times you will have gleaned the target's name by doing your own research, using the methods espoused previously in this chapter. When a person you contact as a result of your research asks you who referred her name, likewise, you must make her feel comfortable that you can keep her name confidential, should she provide you with a referral. How do you do that?

You do this by telling her the truth. You inform her that you utilized the services of a researcher to do the contact name research. By the way, what you are stating is correct. Who did the research? You did, so that makes you a researcher.

Along the same vein, start all research projects by first saying out loud, "I am a researcher, and I pledge that as a researcher I will keep all my sources confidential." There you go—you are a now a bona fide researcher who keeps your sources confidential!

When you are faced by the question "Where did you get my name?" You can now honestly say with total confidence. "My researcher explained to me that based on his research you are a professional who is an expert in X, and that you would be a great source of knowledge. My researcher demands that I keep every professional referral source confidential. As a professional yourself, I hope you can understand that when you provide me with a referral, I will show you the same professional courtesy, and keep every referral confidential, unless you state otherwise. Bottom line, from one professional to another, I really can use your help and I hope I can extend you the same professional courtesy now, or some day if you require assistance. Please jot down my name and number, and if there is anything I can do for you, please do not hesitate to call. Can you provide me with the X names I really need?" Believe me, this approach really works.

Should you receive some resistance—that is, you are not getting the referral you need, and you are in desperate need of help—pull out the "truth trump card" and lay it on the line.

There is nothing wrong with being honest and saying something like "I can appreciate you are a little resistant. I am a voice out of the blue, and you do not know me, but I would not be calling you unless your help was really needed. I am a valuable asset and believe me, I will be a great resource to the company that hires me. I know things are going to break open for me soon. For my children's sake, and my family's sake, I just want it to happen sooner rather than later. I hope you can understand that, as I want to take the pain and anxiety of uncertainty off their faces. You never know, the information you provide could be the key that makes that happen. If you have some contacts or information you can provide now, it is appreciated; if not, can you give it some serious thought and I can call you back? Can you give me a time and day when I can reach you over the next week? If you prefer, I can call you at home." It is important that you come from the heart, rather than from a whining tone. Make sure you keep your tone optimistic and show the person how he or she can be a key factor in helping a family out.

Imagine how a person would feel who had provided you with a contact that led to you getting the job you want. Image how this person would feel when you sent him a picture of your girl, Jane, with a big smile and holding a trophy.

Along with the picture the enclosed note would contain the following: "Thanks to you, Bill, as I wrote you two years ago, your contact led me to my new job, which allowed me to get Jane back into Dressage. Without your help, we could never have afforded the horse, and all the training required. Here are two tickets for all the Dressage events at the Olympics, and airplane tickets to London. Jane will be competing on the national team, and we would like you and your wife to be our guests for the week in London. Jane insists you be there, so fortunately ☺ you have no choice, Bill, and you must accept. This time your country is calling on you to step up and to support an Olympian. God bless you, Bill. Without your help, none of this would have been possible."

Often, appealing to people's humaneness by giving full disclosure of your circumstances will get you results. I have used "truth from the heart" in order to ask for business from my clients when faced with horrible business conditions during two earlier recessions in my career. Believe me, I also struggled over asking for help. I used to believe that asking for help was a sign of weakness.

The circumstances were a high-unemployment economy where our services as headhunters were not in demand, and we were suffering badly. I, like every businessperson at the time, had to pay the bills. I told my clients the truth—that I was ready to get vaporized—and they happily came to the rescue by providing business. I got preferential treatment, because over the years I had made goodwill deposits with my clients.

If you have made goodwill deposits to the universe over your life, do not be afraid to make a withdrawal. Often the best givers are terrible receivers, and as such never would ask for help when in serious need, especially men. Unfortunately the macho effect comes into play for men. This is about giving other people the opportunity to feel the joy of giving. By not asking for help, or not being willing to receive help, it could be argued that one is being selfish. Why? You are robbing people of the good feeling they receive from giving to you.

Getting Contact Information: Telephone Numbers and E-Mails

Once you have your list of names, you will need contact information. Later in the chapter you will be using this information to contact hiring managers directly by telephone, e-mail, or both.

Telephone numbers

You can get most telephone numbers off the company's Website, or use Argali.com ("The most complete and reliable search of telephone directories on the Internet").

E-mail addresses

You have a contact name. How do you get an e-mail address? Most companies have a pattern to their e-mails. Once you figure out the pattern, you are off to the races. E-mail addresses have two parts: the "local part" or user name, which comes before the "at" symbol (@), and the domain name, which comes after the @. For example, in the address jsmith@domain.com, jsmith is the local part (user name) and domain.com is the domain name. The domain name for a company is usually pretty easy to figure out. Just go to the company's Website.

User names can come in a number of configurations, the most common being:

Jsmith, John.Smith, John_Smith, JohnSmith, SmithJohn, Smith.John, Smith_John.

A good way to determine a company's e-mail pattern is to use a common name and do a search on a search engine like Bing or Google. For example, type this search string into Bing: *@**bmo.com** +jeff.

The search results will highlight the e-mail results in Bing and clearly show a pattern of firstname.lastname@bmo.com.

Wink.com

You can also often get social media information about your target name/hiring manager and sometimes an e-mail address by using Wink, or you can get social media contact information. From there you can contact the hiring manager through one of the social sites.

Which Level of Hiring Authority Should You Contact?

The hiring authority you want to contact is usually the second manager up the line from your would-be boss if you are hired. For instance, if you are an analytical chemist then the manager of analytical chemistry is the first level, and the second level is the director of analytical chemistry. The director is who you want to call. The idea is if you are passed down by the director to the manager, there is a stamp of authority on you, and the manager typically views the introduction as a vote of confidence from the director for you.

PRESENTATION MARKETING

You are now in a position to start using the contact names you have gathered and listed to actively connect with them, with the objective of generating meetings, or interviews, with hiring managers. Presentation marketing is presenting your profile directly to a hiring manager. There are four ways to accomplish this:

→ By telephone

→ By e-mail (not preferred in this case)

→ By telephone message followed up by an e-mail

→ In person

No matter how you choose to deliver your direct marketing message, you *must* prepare a punchy, compelling marketing script.

If you cannot bring yourself to make telephone calls for whatever reason, still invest the time now to develop a script that you can then use later for an e-mail campaign. (E-mailing is not the recommended strategy in this case; see "Engagement Marketing" later in the chapter for an e-mail strategy.)

It is best to get an oversight of the whole system first, so read through this whole section once before you start putting together your official script. Then come back and review once more, and then you can put together your script and start making your calls.

The Ingredients for a Dynamite Script

Prepare, prepare, practice, and practice some more—while you are shining up your script. Make sure it feels comfortable. Write it down and make sure you can deliver it with ease. At first when you make calls, you will stumble. It is normal to be a bit off. The goal, however, is to work on your delivery so that you have a smooth start, followed by good flow, *without* any guttural sounds. Use your SCA as the framework for your presentation.

Identify yourself and the reason for your call

Always identify yourself and the purpose of your call. Avoid using a tricky initial delivery, or a slick opening line. It does not work when used on me, or any employer that I know. Instead, just jump right into your delivery. Avoid asking, "Are you available to speak?" or "Is this a good time?" or something similar. The person will tell you if it is not convenient to talk. Furthermore, your time is just as valuable as his time, regardless of whether you are employed or evaluating your career options. You are just as important as anyone else on earth. Make sure you act like it; hold your head high and speak with confidence.

Oversight of your accomplishments and your professional specialty

Here you want to grab her attention with your professional identity, and a quick summary of your most significant accomplishment(s). It is your "wow" statement.

Substantiated impressions others have of you

It is always easy to say you are great at this or that, but when you can back it up through other people's eyes, it has real validity. One of the best ways is through your performance reviews. Always keep copies of your performance reviews. If your manager will not provide them, write down what your manager has given you vocally, and get him or her to sign it. Otherwise, get testimonials on LinkedIn from people you have worked with, or know you in business, and use those in your script.

Significant differentiators/competencies

Select a differentiator that would show that you are special or have a competency cherished by the company or target you are connecting with (for example, you can share or impart your knowledge to others, such as leadership, mentoring, coaching, training, and/or some other impactful differentiator you can point to).

Versatility/volunteering—something beyond your job description

Every manager wants someone who is willing to volunteer, jump in and help, and go above and beyond his or her job description. Managers also love an employee who demonstrates the ability to be flexible and available.

Recognition of others

It is not just all about you. Other people lead to your success, no matter where you work. The ability to give recognition to others is viewed as a real builder of team spirit. A high performer who does not give recognition is viewed as a prima donna, and is quickly despised by others. Give recognition and genuine praise. People appreciate it, and in turn people who give compliments are much better regarded and liked than people who criticize without offering solutions. Be positive, be helpful, and offer thanks, and you will be well liked.

Ability to handle technology/new technology: low learning curve

Demonstrate confidence to get in there and learn something new. Show you have done it in the past. Demonstrate you have the resources to take on new technology challenges, and you also are prepared to learn the new technology—no matter what. Demonstrate you have the ability to find the resources, or you have the network you can call on if need be to help you out.

Point out what the employer has to gain by hiring you

This is the most important part of the presentation: **What is in it for him?** Make sure to spell it out as you summarize your delivery in this section.

Subtle communication of competition for your services

You are doing this with a touch of class. You are not coming out and saying "Bob, Bill down the road is offering me $100K. What do you have for me?" That is crass. Let things develop. You are looking to develop a networking opportunity here that will lead to an interview, a referral, or a callback at a later date. A subtle approach is something like, "I am setting up appointments with employers this week and next..."

Ask for the meeting

Always ask for a meeting. Take the initiative. Ask and you will get.

Provide a choice of day and times to choose from

Always provide a fixed choice—that is, two days and times that you are available for a meeting. When you provide two choices, it makes things easy for people. Will that be "blue" or "white"? "Friday or Thursday?" When you leave it up in the air like "Are you available next week?" it causes an immediate easy out and you will most likely get "No, I am not," or "Give me your number, and I will have someone contact you." *No good!* By providing a choice you get people to check their calendar rather than having to find the time they are available, and this is a positive deal closer for you. If they say the choices you gave them do not work, fire back with "How about Thursday or Friday next week, 7:00 a.m. or 4:00 p.m.?" If they do not choose one, chances are they will come back with one that is open to them.

If you get some resistance (you can usually tell by the tone), ask, "Is there any additional information or questions you would like to ask me that would make you feel more comfortable in setting up a meeting?"

Another comeback I have used successfully is this: "It will take you less energy and time to say yes than it will to banter back and forth with me now and on the next call I make, about reasons why it is not a good time to meet with me. You will also get my e-mails and voice messages, which all take time. Instead why don't we use the time we would be wasting on calls, messages, and e-mails constructively? I will make sure to guarantee that you will benefit greatly from a 15-minute meeting."

If there is total resistance, then at that point, ask him if he knows of anyone within his company that potentially could use your services. If no, ask if he knows anyone outside the company that could use your services. Finally, ask him if he would like a quick profile by e-mail and a list of references he can check, and if it is okay to follow up with him at the same time next week.

Consider that if you back down quickly without a fight, you are probably not the type of person he wants to hire. Employers want people who are enthusiastic, have backbone, can think on their feet, and are determined. When you call, show you are that person by not backing down, and being persistent.

> As an evaluator of talent for many years, one way I separate the "stars" from the average candidates is by rejecting them quickly. I will say something like "I reviewed your resume and you really do not have the skills or the accomplishments my client is seeking." If the person says, "Oh really, that's too bad," no matter what her skills and accomplishments are, she is toast. If, on the other hand, she comes back with something like "Are you sure you can read?" I know I have a live one.

Here is an example of an effective conventional direct marketing script.

Hi, Bob. My name is Paul Hill, and the reason for my call is to demonstrate how I can be of benefit to you and your team. Bob, in more than five years as a scientist, working for a leading CRO, I have developed more than 35 methods for the quantitation of small molecule drugs, as well as validated these methods using modern chromatography techniques including LC/MS/MS. What is in it for you and your team? Bob, you get a dedicated, high-performing scientist who can lead for you, who can deliver for you under tight deadlines, and who can produce high-quality work for you.

Management has routinely recognized me in my performance reviews as exceeding performance objectives, and as being an excellent team player. In my current position I mentor one junior analytical chemist.

The lab team have nicknamed me "Paul the fixer," because I have been elected as the "go-to" person in the lab when it comes to troubleshooting equipment and instruments. Another important fact you should know is Ron, the junior chemist from our lab, and I were instrumental in bringing the UPLC into operational status to schedule.

I am setting up meetings with employers this week. I am still available Tuesday and Wednesday of this week, at 11:00 a.m. or 1:00 p.m. Are you agreeable that it would be a benefit for you to set up a time so we can talk in person?

In less than 60 seconds you have made quite an impression.

As mentioned (and this bears repeating), be prepared.

Practice the delivery of your telephone script by calling friends and presenting your script to them. Stand up and put a smile on your face when calling. Remember to visualize the outcome you want before each call, and make your move. Get in peak state and you will get the results you visualize. Also remember to use the meditation every night, but especially the night before you will be making marketing calls or you have an interview scheduled.

The direct marketing approach is a numbers game: The more calls you make, the better chances you have of connecting with a person who is hiring, or can provide you with a person who may be hiring.

Leaving a Message

Because many hiring managers hide behind voice mail, you need alternative methods to make noise and get noticed. For that reason you also want a shorter version of your marketing script, a barebones script enabling you to leave a 20-second message with the highlights of your script. Here's an example:

Hi, Bob. My name is Paul Hill, and the reason for my call is to demonstrate how I can be of benefit to you and your team. Bob, in more than five years as a scientist working for a leading CRO, I have developed more than 35 methods for the quantitation of small molecule drugs, using LC/MS/MS. What is in it for you and your team? Bob, you get a dedicated, high-performing scientist who can lead for you, who can deliver for you under tight deadlines, and who can produce high-quality work for you. Management has routinely recognized me in my performance reviews as exceeding performance objectives, and as being an excellent team player. I am setting up meetings with employers this week. I am still available Tuesday and Wednesday of this week, at 11:00 a.m., or 1:00 p.m. Would it benefit you to meet with me? Here is my number, and I will follow up with an e-mail.

The Law of 9

Based on call measurements made in my recruitment business, ADV Advanced Technical Services Inc., it takes on average nine attempts, and at least three actual touches or connects, before someone agrees to meet with you. The three connects/touches can be by telephone, e-mail, or mail, to the same decision-maker before he agrees to meet with you or listen to you. This translates into nine attempts in order to get the three touches necessary to get a meeting.

You must be very persistent, and work hard to get your message in the right hands. Most people quit after one call, regardless if they connect or not. **By being persistent, you establish right away your standing, way above the crowd, and it will get you noticed. Keep calling until you get a yes!**

TURNING E-MAIL INTO A TELEPHONE MESSAGE

If you cannot find a target's telephone number you can always e-mail the person a voice recording. This is a good way to personalize the e-mail by using your computer's voice recorder and attaching an audio file in MP3 format to your e-mail. An audio message is a nice personal touch. When you don't have someone's telephone number this is a good way to turn the e-mail resources you do have into what is in essence a telephone message. Limit your recordings to one minute. This personal approach may make the decision-maker respond even though she has not responded to your other nine calls and e-mails. It is different, unique, and original, and gets results. The bonus is that many decision-makers are always plugged into their e-mail through their smart phones and will access their e-mail many times a day. Voice mail tends to go unattended for many decision-makers.

ALTERNATIVE METHODS THAT GET YOU HIRED

When times are tough, hiring authorities are being bombarded with resumes, e-mails, and calls. The "same old, same old" does not work as well anymore. Old ways of marketing are just not as effective. A persistent direct marketing campaign will pay off; the key is being persistent. Direct marketing won't work if you make only one call to each contact, as most people do, and for those who are not willing to follow through aggressively, you need methods and techniques that will draw in the hiring authority, get him engaged, and effectively get you noticed. As you now know, sending your resume to personnel is not going to cut it. "Clicking and sending" usually won't work. If you are lucky, the e-mailed, boring cover letter followed by a resume might get you an interview, but you will be competing with a 100 others for a job you probably don't really cherish.

What you need are techniques that will eliminate your competition from the get-go!

ENGAGEMENT MARKETING

The premise today is that hiring authorities and the public are jaded. We just do not trust anyone! How do you build trust with a hiring authority? Slowly, through your ProfessionaliBrand, as well as through social networking and by building an online and telephone relationship. The same is true with the GetHiredFastTrack method called engagement marketing. You need an equal amount of touches in engagement marketing in order to build familiarity and trust.

This is a technique I developed that has proven incredibly successful for my clients. Let me be clear: It takes time, effort, and persistence. It is all about building trust. It is less intrusive than a telephone call, and many job-seekers find it a less stressful approach. The objective here is to engage your target in communicating with you, then systematically ramping up their interest and trust in you through a series of e-mails, until they feel compelled or obligated to meet with you or help you out.

> The key to engagement marketing is to remember that less is more!

Why You Need Engagement Marketing if You Are Addicted to "Click and Send"

To make the point that "less is more" is in fact a better strategy, let's consider the typical "click and send" mentality and approach to job search.

As mentioned over and over, most people follow the traditional approach to job search: the dreaded "click and send." Most of you have taken this traditional approach, which involves sending an e-mail haphazardly to hr@WeWontHireYou.com or to careers@ThanksButNoThanks.com, explaining in the body of the e-mail that you have attached your cover letter and resume. Your target, upon reading the body of your email is probably thinking, *Thanks for that insightful e-mail. Had you not told me about those attachments, I would have never known they were there.* Maybe instead, you have written something a little more insightful, like, "I am looking for a job as a technician.

My qualification and personal details are given in the resume attached." Okay, yes, I am being sarcastic. However, it is to make a point:

If you are going to bother saying something, *say something.*

The directors and VPs that I interface with regularly inform me that because of the volume of e-mails they receive, they only take a moment to glance at the subject matter before trashing the e-mail. If there is a resume attached, they tell me they often trash the e-mail without opening it.

Do I have your attention? Do you still want to waste your time with those "resume attached" e-mails?

Engagement marketing is an e-mail approach; follow the techniques described earlier in the chapter to get the e-mail address of the hiring managers you want to target.

Ground Rules for Engagement Marketing

➤ Know what you want.

➤ Identify the right hiring authority.

➤ Follow the strategic approach laid out at the beginning of the chapter. Remember: Nail down your plan by first identifying geography, company type, and level of person to be targeted, and then the actual name of person to be targeted, and get the e-mail address.

➤ Remember to "chunk" your work. Start with one geographical area, five companies, and a maximum of 30 names with corresponding e-mail addresses.

➤ Do not provide a resume or cover letter. The idea is to hold off the hiring manager to allow you time to build a rapport first. Even if she requests a resume right after she receives your first e-mail, make sure to stall by, for example, offering up references instead. Once you let your resume out of the bag, communication tends to stop. **Remember: A resume does not get you hired—you do!** The objective is to give the hiring manager more and more of *you,* and much less resume. By the end of your exchange you want her to know who you are.

➤ The engagement process should flow in a controlled manner, where you are the conductor of the e-mail flow.

➤ Make sure to pick a subject that will be attention-grabbing in your first e-mail.

An example of an engagement marketing exchange

Use the scripts that follow to tailor your approach according to your specialty or the job you are targeting. The premise is you are a business development specialist for a Phase I Contract Research Services Company. In the following example, each exchange is an e-mail.

Subject: Increasing Phase I sales in a down sales market

> **You:** "I know everyone is struggling to increase sales. Let me share with you a technique I used successfully to generate $15 million in Phase I sales last year for XXX [put a competitor's name here]. Would you would like more information on how you can significantly increase your revenues by using this approach?"
>
> **Target:** "Yes, please share that with me."

If you did not get a response to the original e-mail, start the next e-mail with "I sent you an e-mail on [date], and this is to follow up that e-mail." Change the subject line to something attention-grabbing like: **"Phase I— Avoid a sales disaster."**

> **You:** *Give a brief outline of the description of your approach, without giving everything.* "Do you believe this approach would be beneficial to your company?"
>
> **Target:** "Yes, I do, thank you for sharing."
>
> **You:** "I am starting to explore opportunities with a select few companies that I believe I can help. Your company seems very attractive. Do you consistently look to improve your team by adding top performers, or replacing non-performers with top performers?"
>
> **Target:** "Yes, we do. Please send me your resume."
>
> **You:** "I am currently working on the finishing touches of the resume. I am setting up meetings with employers and contacts that I have in the industry for next week. I am still available Tuesday and Wednesday of next week at 11 a.m. or 1 p.m. Are you agreeable that it would be beneficial for us to set up a time to talk in person (if you are local) or by the phone (if long distance)? I can bring in my resume with me at that point, or if you prefer a call, I can send it to you prior to the call."

If you get a positive response, make sure to brush up on preparing for an interview. (See Chapter 10.)

Target: No response.

Wait two days, and then follow up with:

You: "To follow up on our last communication, please find a list of my major accomplishments. Would you like a list of my references?"

Target: "Yes. Please send your references."

You: "Tuesday and Wednesday are now booked. What about Thursday or Friday next week, 7 a.m., or 4 p.m.?"

Target: "Confirmed for Friday at 4 p.m. Please call me at (416) 933-1883."

Great. You have a call confirmed. In the event that this not the case and you still have no response from your target then follow up with:

You: "Please find some excerpts from my performance reviews."

If still no response, follow up with:

You: "I have been expecting to hear back from you. To view my online resume and video resume please follow the link. I will follow up on Wednesday at 8 a.m. [be specific] by telephone."

If still no response, follow up with:

You: "Bob, I am very interested in your company. Is there anyone within your company that you can refer me to? Please provide me with his contact information." [Add a link to your online resume again or attach a PDF version of your resume.]

Still no response:

You: "Bob, I know you are very knowledgeable in the industry, and have many contacts. From one professional to another, can you refer me to anyone outside your company? If I can be of any help with respect to a resource for you or your staff, please call on me about anything. I look forward to hearing from you, and I hope my sales approach turns out to be a good addition for you and your team."

Remember to add a button to your e-mail signature and one to your online resume that contains your video resume as well and at least one button for LinkedIn. It has been demonstrated that the bigger the button or advertisement/badge on a Website, the more people click; this was confirmed in a number of online studies. Ever notice those Groupon adverts on sites? Give it a try and you will find some great results.

An alternative is to open with an accomplishment that will resonate with your target.

Customize or adjust the preceding example as you see fit. With a bit of tweaking, you will get the response and outcome you want.

> Be persistent. Do not give up after a few steps. If you do not get a response, give it one day and follow through with the sequence until you have laid it out to the last e-mail. You cannot assume your target is not interested in you. Perhaps she is traveling or away from work, or there is something preventing her from responding. Be courteous and positive. If you have followed through and nothing happens, wrap it up and move on. If you are diligent and you do follow up, chances are you will in turn receive a follow-up call sometime in the future. It has been my experience with clients that eventually the effort pays dividends.

The next question is: Are you marketing to a target that is actively looking and has a confirmed need for someone with your competencies, or are you marketing to a target that has no *initial* interest in hiring you? How do you target buyers and how do you turn a non-buyer, non-interested decision-maker into a buyer/hirer?

Increasing the Odds by Marketing to Buyers

At any one point in time, as Chet Holmes says in Anthony Robbins's "The Money Master Series" audio series, only 3 percent of the population is actually in the market for any particular product or service (tires, furniture, carpet cleaning, and so forth). Because 3 percent is a very limited marketplace, the challenge to a marketer is this: How do you convert some of the remaining 97 percent "non-needers" into "wanters" of your product or service?

For the sake of argument, let us extrapolate this a bit and extend a "service" to mean your services as an employee. In the best of worlds if Chet Holmes is correct, and you targeted 100 hiring managers, only three would actually be in the market for your services at any one time. Any way you slice it those are pretty sad numbers.

How Many Cold Calls or Cold E-Mails Does it Actually Take?

Let's look at the numbers based on the statistics quoted earlier from my recruitment business. **It takes three attempts to get one touch and it takes three touches to get a meeting, so therefore it takes nine touches to get a meeting.**

Most seasoned headhunters typically would be making 50 cold calls per day. Because most likely you are not a seasoned sales professional, how many calls would you need to make, and to how many managers or executives, over how many days in order to get in front of a decision-maker who is actually in need of your services? If we use the 27 attempts to get a meeting, and the 3-percent rule of an executive being in the market for someone like you, you would need to make 33.33 calls per day, to the same 33.33 executives every day, over 27 days—to gain 33.33 meetings—and *only one* of these executives would actually be in need of your services. Therefore, only one meeting has the potential to pay off. **Thirty-three calls a day, for 27 days, to the same 33 executives, just to find *one* who is actually in need of your services!** That is actually about 900 calls over 27 days, or a little more than four work weeks of straight calls. No wonder that job-seekers are so dismayed by the process of finding a job by cold calling.

How Do You Substantially Increase Those Odds?

The preferred way is to be first in mind and go after the real hidden job market, as you have already learned. Alternatives do exist. You can also increase your odds of getting hired by marketing to hiring managers who are actually seeking someone like you and also by using fear-based marketing to open doors.

Increase Your Odds of Marketing to a Buyer

To increase your odds of marketing to someone who has indicated an actual need, and is most likely hiring, use a job spider like *www.indeed.com*. A job spider is a search engine for jobs, allowing job-seekers to find jobs posted on thousands of company career sites and job boards. The best way to use Indeed.com is to save your initial search parameters. Indeed.com will automatically deliver the new openings to your e-mail inbox every day.

As a result of using Indeed you will turn up many corporate advertisements instructing you to respond to the ad by applying through a general e-mail box or an HR e-mail. Avoid responding in this fashion. Be aware that all jobs are not necessarily real, and by going to the source if it exists you save time and heartache by following a more direct and better protocol.

The better protocol to follow is to find the hiring manager's name, using the techniques discussed in this book. Approach him with the type of preparation and marketing technique that is most appropriate for your situation. This way you bust through the crowd and get in on top.

Use Indeed.com most effectively by using the Advanced Job Search link right below the main search box (*www.indeed.com/advanced_search*). Select "Show jobs" from the drop-down menu, "Employer websites only," and check the "Exclude staffing agencies" box. You get a much cleaner search, and of course you get the names of the companies you can approach directly. You also eliminate the job boards, where everyone who is looking for a job tends to congregate, as well as the staffing agencies. Once you run one search, provide your e-mail in order to receive daily updates sent to your mailbox.

FEAR-BASED EDUCATION MARKETING

Increase your buyer market by going after the 97 percent and converting them into buyers.

If the "need" market is only 3 percent at any one time, how do you get *more than 3 percent* of the market to become buyers? How do you convert decision-makers who have no perceived need for your services into decision-makers who want to hire you?

Again I turn to Chet Holmes—this time his book *The Ultimate Sales Machine*. I sum up his marketing tactic as "Target only the best companies with fear-based education marketing, and back up your fear-based education offering with implied social proof."

A good way to explain this is by using an example. Let's say you are a senior scientist with a passion for working for independent pharmaceutical contract research organizations. Approach your target with the following type of script. Begin your script with a fear-based, attention-grabbing subject in order to capture your contact's attention.

My name is Joe Perfect employee, and the reason for my call is I have prepared a white paper called "What Your Competitors Are Doing Now to Drive You out of Business." Throughout the last 10 years, I have been helping contract research companies become more successful, and make more money. I have learned there are some pretty serious and significant challenges facing contract research companies coming up over the next years. Because my passion is tied with the reputable and successful independents in the CRO industry, I wanted you to have every opportunity to be ahead of these upcoming problems which will definitely hit the industry.

I present this important white paper in a very succinct format to all the top independent CROs. In fact, I am in touch with [enter names of competitors], and I am in the process of arranging presentations during a management meeting. I'd love to guarantee that you also see for yourself this very important information. Is finding out how to avoid going out of business something you are interested in? Are you available next week to see me on Tuesday at 10 a.m. or Thursday at 9:30 a.m.?

Breaking Down the Script

As you can see:

➡ Fear is used by invoking the words *driving you out of business.*

➡ Education is being offered, through a white paper in this case.

➡ Social proof is being invoked because it is being inferred that competitors are considering, or have set up meetings to view, the presentation. "Social proof" validates the presentation as being valuable.

Once they hear your presentation and meet with you, you can move the conversation toward the need to hire you in order to mitigate the dangers.

You do not have to write a white paper. You can find all kinds of research on the Internet to substantiate a series of claims on a subject that could be packaged in a fear-based format, and then communicated by you to your target. **Of course the central idea is that you are the hero that can swoop in (get hired) and save the day.**

Another Fear-Based Education Example

You are a building maintenance manager, and you prepare a cold call script in which you ask to meet the general manager of a plant to discuss "the five most dangerous and neglected aspects of building management that have caused an exponential rise in litigation losses" or "the seven most deadly health hazards in commercial buildings today and how they are effecting your health in a precipitously detrimental way—even in as little time as it takes to read this headline." Use fear-based marketing to "shake up" decision-makers into hiring you.

OUTRAGEOUS POSTCARDS, MARKETING LETTERS, AND SNAIL MAIL

One of the effective methods to get a hiring manager's attention is to use the mail—not e-mail, but snail mail. With all the electronic bombardment we get today very few of us pay much attention to what comes into our inbox.

When I ask most professionals if they still open their mail, and this includes decision-makers, the answer is always yes. You need to take advantage of this in your job search. Instead of sending along boring hard copy of your resume, why not get innovative by using outrageous, eye-popping postcards with a link to your video resume or your iResumePro?

Get cute, get funny, and get outrageous. One postcard that we used was a picture of a great white shark leaping into the air from the ocean. On the flip side of the card was the title "Collection Manager ready to hunt down what's yours" with a caption that said, "If you are seeking a fish out of water don't call me, but if you are seeking a shark in fish-infested waters check out my iVideo-ResumePro and give me a call." We provided a link to the iVideoResumePro and a telephone number as well. Bottom line: It has worked wonders.

Getting creative with your mail marketing campaign and using the video resume in your marketing efforts can also save a lot of time for both parties. You can order postcards online, and have them professionally printed and back to you within three days. I recommend using oversized, 6 x 11 postcards. (Go to *www.transitiontohired.com/resources* to get information.)

Marketing Letter

You can also use the marketing letter with a link to your video resume as an effective strategy. Remember: You do not enclose your traditional, printed resume with this letter. Rather, you simply send the letter with a link to your video resume or LinkedIn profile.

Here is an example of a marketing letter:

Dear employer:

I want to help your company meet its goal of ending world hunger. One of the challenges of a conventional resume, I presume you would agree, is it is not a great medium for you to get a good "picture" or "read" on "me" as a person. I invite you to visit this link *www.projectmanagerboston.com/ivideoresumepro*, where you will find a short video and you can get to know me. My hope is you will get a much better understanding of my personality, my presentation skills, my competencies, my accomplishments, and my communication abilities.

I believe I am well suited to producing compelling results as a Project Manager. My compensation target is in the $80–95K a year range and I would welcome a call after you review my iVideoResumePro.

I can be reached at (123) 456-7890 weekdays between 6 a.m. and 9 a.m., and evenings after 7 p.m.

Thank you.

Choose bright white quality paper, 100% cotton, and 24 pound paper. **Do not use recycled copy paper.** Have your letter professionally printed. Spend the extra money to get a quality envelope as well as stamps that you apply manually. Address the envelopes by hand. Do not use a standard #10 business envelope; it has "resume" written all over it. Instead, use a card-sized envelope or an unusual size with corresponding paper to fit. Blend old-school with new-school, be innovative, and persist, and you will be amazed at the results.

BECOMING A FREE AGENT OR CONTRACTOR

The No-Risk Guarantee

"Mr. Employer, if you are not totally satisfied, then don't pay me." A bold statement that works to get you work, and you *do* get paid.

According to the U.S. Census Bureau, "about three quarters of all U.S. business firms have no payroll. Most are self-employed persons operating unincorporated businesses...."[3] If 75 percent of businesses in the United States are one-person small businesses (businesses without payroll), which could be argued is just another form of contracting, this means there is a major trend shift taking place in America, from full-time jobs to embracing free agency or contracting as a way of life. The "perfect storm" is building against full-time secure employment, and it is important that you realize it. The forces are gathering, with the shift to project-based hiring (outsourcing and offshoring) as evidenced by the success of the myriad successful project-based sites like Elance.com and Guru.com. Add globalization and the selection and reach employers have through the Web, as well as a trend just starting toward "shift and wage bidding," and I hope you can see the alarming need to take action by having your contracting/consulting hat at the ready. You need a flexible and fall-back option you can count on for income production, because that glorious full-time job may never present itself again. "Be Irresistible" and guarantee your income by embracing the new realities of competition and globalization.

Different Times Require Aggressive Methods of Getting Work

Instead of fighting the trend, join it. Increase your employability by using fear-based education marketing to open the doors for you, and offer your services for free to the hiring authority (or hiring authorities) that you are a valuable asset. Offer to work for free on a project for three months, and tell the employer if they are not happy with your services not to pay a cent. Prior to starting, draw up an employment contract that states your fee for performance, as well as your guarantee. Have the agreement authorized by the employer.

As a New Graduate Take the Same Approach

If you cannot wrap your head around the fear-based marketing approach, an alternative is to identify potential problems that you can solve for the company. You contact the appropriate decision-maker, propose to fix the problem, and offer to work on a pay-for-performance basis. You offer to work and get paid only when a project is complete to the company's satisfaction. As a recent graduate in a tough market you need to embrace short-term, "let me prove myself to you." My view is that in the coming years it will be common or even necessary to create your own job. In order to get the work it will be necessary to be passionate about it. Otherwise, if you are only in it for the money, someone with passion will beat you out.

Having made the contacts or attracted interest, you will still, in most cases, have to go through the "poking and prodding" phase of pre-employment: the interview—or what I like to call the LKTH dance (Like you, get to Know you, Trust you, and Hire you).

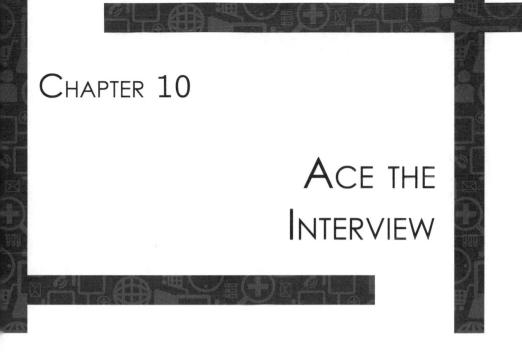

Chapter 10

Ace the Interview

"Few have strength of reason to overrule the perceptions of sense, and yet fewer have curiosity or benevolence to struggle long against the first impression. He who therefore fails to please in his salutation and address, is at once rejected, and never obtains an opportunity of showing his latest excellences or essential qualities."

—Samuel Johnson[1]

Telephone Interview

When you are successful in getting a hiring manager seriously interested in you, your next hurdle will most likely be responding to a telephone interview request by an "in-house" corporate human resources recruiter.

If you have been invited to a telephone interview, this indicates they like your competencies as related through your profile online or through a great ProfessionaliBrand, or maybe even through a traditional resume. It is now up to you to get the job.

If you have not prepared for the telephone interview, then you will not get the invite to an in-person or video interview. (Go to *www.transitiontohired.com/resources* to get information on how to prepare for a telephone interview.) If you have prepared, then you probably prepared poorly. There is no excuse for preparing poorly.

You put all that effort into getting to the interview stage. It would now be a downer if you let the opportunity slip away because you did not practice and prepare for the interview. Just like any other skill, interviewing can be mastered.

A telephone interview will most likely focus on "soft skills." The team in human resources is required to do their job and their assessment. A conversation with you will give them some insight on:

➔ Energy/enthusiasm

➔ Passion

➔ Ambition/initiative/drive

➔ Level of research conducted on the hiring company

➔ Listening skills

➔ Interest level

Always make sure to conduct a telephone interview from a quiet place with no possible interruptions. Never conduct a telephone interview while on a cell phone or in a noisy environment, from an area that does not allow for privacy, or while driving. Any of these situations will affect the outcome of your interview. Many times in my work as a headhunter, the most common feedback about telephone interview candidate failure from the employer would be "I could not really get a good take on his communication skills because the connection was so bad. I think I will pass on him." Even though our candidates were well schooled on how to conduct proper interviews, they still took calls on their cell phones or in environments where they were interrupted. Heed the advice or suffer the consequences!

COMPANY RESEARCH, RESEARCH ON INTERVIEWER'S PROFILE, AND FORMULATING QUESTIONS

With the era of "Google-iscious" amounts of information at your finger-tips, it is unforgivable not to have researched the employer prior to an interview. It is imperative that you do thorough research on the employer. In most cases, you should be able to find information and a profile on the person or people who will be interviewing you. To this end, when confirming the interview, ask for an interview agenda with the interviewer's/interviewers' names. If an agenda is not available, ask for at least the name(s). Tell the interview scheduler (usually a human resources specialist) that you want to prepare adequately for the interview. This will also serve to demonstrate to the human resources team that you are taking the opportunity seriously and that you are a conscientious professional. A positive review from human resources could just be the extra push needed to get you hired, should a tight race for the job develop.

Get a good grasp of the company, the job, and the people involved before the interview. Having this knowledge allows you to formulate well-thought-out questions that will impress your interviewers.

During client debriefs, I have often heard feedback such as "Things went well. He answered all the questions we asked of him. However, he had no questions. Either he was not listening, not interested, or did not understand anything we said. We even asked him three times at the end of the interview if he had any questions. It just seemed like he wanted to get out of here, like he had something more important to do." When I or my staff debried these can-didates, it never failed; they said something like "I really want this job." When providing the client's feedback to the candidate, and asking the candidate why questions were not asked, the answer was always something like "I did not know what to ask." When you asked the candidate if he read the information you sent him on the company, and the interviewers' profiles, or had he done extra research on his own, he usually had said something like "I did not think it was important" or "I was too busy" or something similar. The end result was he did not get the job he wanted—nor will you if you do the same. What a crying shame! Do your homework.

Position Knowledge and Position Objective

Having a good understanding of the position's objective or knowing what main problem the interviewer(s) is trying to solve by hiring someone is the key to having a great interview. Having this information gives you a great advantage, because you can practice and prepare answers that will directly address this objective, by drawing on your past experience.

If you cannot get this information pre-interview and/or the hiring manager cannot articulate it during the interview, you can bring it to the forefront by asking this: "Why don't we look at this together? So I am clear, can we nail down what major outcomes need to be achieved in this position and by when?" This approach will get you noticed. (More information is provided on this approach in this chapter.)

Taking Control of the Interview: Guiding the Interview to Your Advantage

One of the most powerful ways to get your knowledge in front of the interviewer is to really understand what she needs. Many times an interviewer does not know or she has a preconceived view that letting you know what she is looking for puts her at a disadvantage. Personally, I prefer giving the questions to the candidate prior to the interview, so he can prepare to show me where he has the necessary competencies to solve the problems at hand. Yet most interviewers will act as if they are holding the secret recipe to Coca-Cola in their grubby hands. If you want to show your best colors, you need to know what colors your interviewer needs and wants in order to satisfy her objectives.

In my corporate recruiting practice at ADV through the years, we have taught the following interview tactics to our candidates with great results. One aspect of our responsibilities is to facilitate interviews between clients and candidates. When sitting in on these interviews and facilitating the exchange I have seen firsthand how these tactics dramatically and positively impact an interview in a candidate's favor. I first learned about tactical interviewing from my first supervisor in the head hunting business, Tony Grillo. I subsequently adapted the tactics to the GetHiredFastTrack methodology.

Continuous Improvement Tactic

The tactic in this situation is to appeal to the manager's "continuous improvement" mentality. Every manager wants a better employee. Guide the interview with a question such as this: "Mr. Potential Boss, if you look back on this job and how it has been done in the past, and if you could change some things about how it was done, what would you do to make it better?"

By asking a question like this, you are uncovering what the manager considers great performance standards for this position. The strategy for you is to take these answers and demonstrate how your skills, abilities, and past performance will enable you to meet or exceed these "make it better" performance standards. In other words, what competencies does the manager view as "needed" to be outstanding in the job?

Ideal Candidate Tactic

The tactic is to get the interviewer to tell you what he considers to be the ideal characteristics (style, behavior) of the new employee.

Because of what we discussed previously regarding the guarded secrets mentality, you usually cannot come out at the start of the interview with the question, "Mr. Potential Boss, can you describe to me the ideal candidate for this job?"

Usually the response would be something like: "Sure, Mr. To-Remain-Unemployed, in another life."

You need to use a little skill, start up a dialogue, and rephrase the question so it is not as obvious.

For example, you might say: "Can you think back to someone who was great in the job, or is now great in the job? What characteristics would you say make or made him the best?"

Alternatively, you can take a more direct approach: "Mr. Potential Boss, is it important for you to get the best candidate possible for this position? You agree this is important? Because you agree, does it make sense for you to find out if I am the ideal match that you require? In order to be able to demonstrate to you that I have those ideal competencies, do you think it makes sense that I know what they are before I start the interview, so when I answer your questions I can point out specifically those areas that will match, or not match your competency requirements?"

When you have this input, you can keep it in mind when formulating your answers during the interview, therefore demonstrating with precision that you are the ideal candidate.

The great advantage of knowing what makes the ideal candidate is that both parties can walk away knowing it is a match rather than walking away thinking "maybe," or guessing.

Predicting Future Needs

The tactic is to first recognize that companies are always looking to improve any number of things. It could be a product, a process, customer service relationships, or marketing—you name it, pretty well everything. How can you use this to your advantage?

First, you need to find out what major objectives the department, company, or manager wants to achieve in the next year or more. It is important to show how you can meet those objectives, and even go beyond them, by uncovering and pointing out needs they will have that they are not even aware of yet or that they have not even planned for yet. It's also a great time to pull out a fear-based question, such as: "Have you considered a pre-emptive strike to counter what your competitors are doing right now to put you out of business?" Believe me, this gets everyone's attention.

Here's an example of a more subtle approach: You interview for a marketing and customer relations manager position for a small company. It is owned by an "old style" owner who believes marketing requires good ads in newspapers and magazines, for the cheapest possible rate, attending trade shows, designing fancy print brochures, and having 10 customer relationship people answering basic questions like "Where do I send the products for repair?" or "Where can I get replacement parts?"

You show how you can meet the basics requirements of the job (designing brochures, organization trade shows, and managing a customer relations group). However, after establishing the basics, you ask: "Have you considered how you can increase your sales dramatically, and cut down your costs, by using newer-style marketing strategies, yet keep the older-style touch and feel that is important to your company?"

All of a sudden you are not just answering questions like everyone else, but you are looking to the future to some areas the owner may never have even thought of.

When he asks for more information, you might say something like this: "I know keeping the personal touch is important through your customer relations staff. I also know that sending out conventional marketing brochures by post is important to you. I can tell that you want to increase sales yet preserve "personal touch." Are you open to hearing about ways you can achieve both?

You have a large team of customer relations people that could be deployed in a much better fashion that would result in increasing sales and customer loyalty. Your Website could have a simple addition of frequently asked questions. This would cut down the volume of calls. Alternatively, I would deploy the extra freed-up manpower to contact new customers to make sure they are happy with their purchase. At the same time, our customer relations team would inform customers where they can find specific information 24/7 on the Website, as well as point out complementary products that they may be interested in purchasing. I would also recommend that we offer these customers 20% off their next purchase, and should a new customer be recommended by them, we would offer a discount to that new customer also.

I know you do not believe in this e-mail marketing stuff, and I agree with you that it is less effective today. However, by installing a CRM system, we can capture much more information online, as well as at the point of sale and therefore be able to target our customers in an automated manner. An integrated system would prepare brochures for mailing as well as automate the sending of e-mail offers. With a good CRM system we can also personalize customer communications, preserving the personal touch. For example, we send out three brochures during the two weeks prior to a customer's birthday hoping that the wife, husband, partner, or children will see the brochure and be motivated to buy a birthday gift from us, because the intended recipient is already a fan of our products. Furthermore, we take two of our customer service team and train them in social media best practices in order to engage customers in discussions about our products, as well as share information with these customers to influence them in their purchase decisions and use this shared information to convince the "purse string holder" of the value of a purchase from us.

Of all the tactics, this one will really makes the employer take notice, and it is the one that I recommend as the most important out of all of the great interview tactics. Do your homework and uncover the employer's future "pain points." Open the wound, show them how to apply the bandage, and get hired so you can implement a full rehabilitation and growth process.

The Biggest Problem Tactic

The reason the position is open is because the interviewer or the company has a problem it wants solved. Frequently interviews revolve around finding out your qualifications and skills, rather than what actually needs to be done.

In my role as a headhunter, I was frequently given job descriptions that required a PhD for education. When I probed and asked, "Why do you require a PhD?" the answer was, "Because the job requires it." When I asked again by rephrasing the question to "What specifically in the duties, responsibilities, and objectives of the position require a PhD in education in order to fulfill the requirements?" the answer I invariably got was this: "Because we do. That has always been the requirements of the position."

"Are you saying that there is no way a BS could do the job?"

"Well, I guess they could."

"Do you think it would make sense to review the job requirements at this point?"

I would then go on to say, "Mr. Employer, what if you started by asking the following question: What problems do I need solved? Once you have the answer to that question, then ask: What compentencies does my new employee need to possess in order to be competent in solving these problems? Do you think this would be a better way to get the answers you need to get the job done?"

The outcome, of course, of this exercise, for employers that did not get all their feathers ruffled, was to rethink their approach and agree to rewrite a new job description with me. For those that did not, they ended up hiring a PhD who then quit and they were invariably back to square one every six months to a year. This is why it is critical for you to understand the job. You need a job that fits you; otherwise you will quit or be fired. It is therefore of prime importance to know how you can get the job description figuratively re-written during the interview.

Just ask a simple question like this: "What problems would you like to see tackled and resolved in the next three months, six months, one year? And looking further out to the next two years?" Once you have these answers, you can tailor your answer to fit the requirements and/or decide if this job is for you or not.

The Hurdle Tactic

This is a little different tactic. What you are looking for here are the impediments that could/would stop a person from achieving the stated targets or solving the problems that need solving. Once you know what the interviewer perceives as the hurdles to success, you can point out how you can overcome those hurdles and succeed.

For example, a question like this would be effective: "What do you see as the potential roadblocks to success in solving the problems we just discussed?"

PREPARE TO ASK QUESTIONS DURING THE INTERVIEW

I cannot stress strongly enough how important it is to prepare and formulate questions before the interview, based on the extensive research that you conducted.

It is also important to be an active listener. Bring a notebook and jot down points as the interview goes along in order to jog your memory so you can formulate questions and ask them when the appropriate opportunity presents itself. Avoid taking constant notes, as you want to focus your attention on listening and keeping eye contact. Jot down a few keywords to jog your memory, and trust you will remember.

Prepare the bulk of your questions in advance of the interview. Some we have already touched on, but require re-emphasis because of their importance. Use the questions that follow as a guide to help you formulate your specific questions. By getting answers to these or similar questions, you will be in a better position to make an informed decision regarding the opportunity, and point out where your skills and abilities can best be maximized.

Some questions are more pertinent to a second interview or even just prior to accepting an offer; the bottom line is you should have these answers prior to accepting a position.

Questions About the Position Responsibilities and Objectives

Use the following questions to formulate your specific questions. Obviously if the questions have already been answered during the interview do not ask again unless you need clarification. Also I am not saying ask all these questions during the interview; get some answers pre-interview through your research or through asking HR, or pre-acceptance.

➤ What are the duties, functions, and responsibilities of the position?

➤ What will your role be?

➤ What is the primary objective of the manager in hiring someone?

➤ What problem does the manager want solved by hiring someone?

➤ What technical issues are important? What business or sales concerns need to be solved?

➤ What will I be doing on a day-to-day basis? (Get the interviewer to describe a typical work day.)

➤ How does the position fit into the "big picture" of what needs to be accomplished by the department, division, and/or company? This will demonstrate to you "how" and "where" you fit into the "whole" of the organization.

➤ Why is the position available?

➤ What are the plans for the department and company? Over one year? Two years? And long-term?

What are the performance standards?

➤ What performance standards define success for this position?

➤ In specific, job-related terms, what critical functions must be performed in order to meet or exceed expectations? What goals/milestones do I need to achieve within three months, six months, and one year, in order to be considered an above-average performer on this team?

➤ How will the performance standards be communicated? Daily? Weekly? Monthly? Quarterly? Annually?

➤ How does the employer or manager do things? What are his or her policies? Rules? Expectations?

➤ What job progression can you expect when you meet the objectives?

Finding out about the manager

➤ What is it like to work for you? You may be surprised by the honest reply you get to this question.

➤ What can I expect from you on a day-to-day basis in terms of guidance, support, and leadership?

➤ What is your management style? Are you a micro-manager or a macro-manager? Do you dictate or are you consultative and open to input? Do you apply metrics, or do you provide general guidance and targets, and get out of the way, and let the person get the job done?

➤ How will we communicate and interface on the job? For example, only at meetings, through daily or weekly reporting, or will we be working side by side? Can you provide me with an example of how this works during a typical day on the job?

HOW TO HANDLE SALARY AND COMPENSATION QUESTIONS

With respect to salary, try not to pin yourself down to a specific number until you have a total and realistic picture of the compensation package. Do not bring up the issue of money until you are asked or until it is brought up. It is important not to dwell on money (unless you are in sales), because the focus should be on the opportunity. Get a true picture of the total opportunity prior to locking into some number. Provide a true picture of your total package if you are asked for your salary. For example: "I make [or made] a base salary of $X plus overtime, stock options, performance bonus, and a share purchase plan, as well as time off in lieu of overtime." This is where being chased after as a candidate because of your great online professional image pays off over being an applicant on his knees hoping to get an offer. As a candidate you have much more leverage than an applicant. Your income depends on your irresistibility, so create a great online presence and reputation through ProfessionaliBranding.

If the interviewer pushes for a specific salary figure that you are seeking, make sure to give the interviewer a range. Remember to consider the whole package, not only the salary, as most companies today are offering structured packages for professionals. These packages can pay off handsomely in the future through stock options, bonuses, and incentives. Find out if any other pay-for-performance bonuses are available.

One of the biggest mistakes a candidate makes during an interview is mentioning a low salary number for fear of not being considered or thinking that by doing so she will seem more attractive to the employer.

After being selected by the employer for an offer, the "chosen one" may rationalize, and rightly so, that the position requires longer hours and entails greater responsibility than first thought. The candidate may try to substantiate a higher salary request than previously asked for, by now bringing up the facts of a recent salary review, stock options, bonuses, or other perks that were not mentioned previously during the interview process. You can bet, however, that the offer from the company will be the lower figure the candidate quoted initially. It is very difficult to change this figure, or adjust it once the cat is out of the bag, so to speak, no matter how much ammunition you throw at it at a later date. Think through your requirements carefully. Make sure that they are realistic.

HOW TO DESCRIBE YOURSELF DURING AN INTERVIEW BASED ON YOUR LEVEL OF SENIORITY

Here is a thought-provoking question for you: If you are a manager, is it important to describe yourself in terms of work ethic, dependability, initiative, ability to work well with others, good time management, and communication skills at an interview or even on your resume? The answer to this question for a manager may surprise you. In order to win at interviews you need to know how to describe yourself based on your level of seniority or the level of seniority of the position. You can get more detailed information on this topic and on interviewing and blow them away at your next interview by going to *www.transitiontohired.com/resources.*

Chapter 11

Close the Deal and Get Hired

"Asking is the beginning of receiving. Make sure you don't go to the ocean with a teaspoon. At least take a bucket so the kids won't laugh at you."

—Jim Rohn[1]

Typically your interviewer will ask if you have any questions at the end of the interview. If you have done a good job of asking questions during the interview, and likewise your questions have been answered satisfactorily, you will not have any questions. Whether you have or you have not asked questions during the interview, this is your cue to take action. You want to demonstrate to the interviewer that you have grasped the important issues, bolster the interviewer's enthusiasm for you, and finally confirm you are the right choice.

Start by repeating or rephrasing the major themes that are important in the job as perceived by the interviewer(s). Next, reassure him or her that you have the right stuff by showing how your abilities and experience are a good match. Finally, ask for the job by confirming you are the ideal candidate. Make sure to describe yourself in a way that is appropriate for your level of seniority. (Visit *www.transitiontohired.com/resources* to get more information on this subject and how to fine-tune your wrap-up.)

CLOSING THE DEAL: FOLLOWING UP

Yes, persistence in follow-up with a handwritten thank-you card sent by mail to each party involved in the interview goes a long way to closing the deal, especially if you are an early contender in the interview sweepstakes. Because interview competitions for professional positions tend go on for more than a month and sometimes longer, my opinion, based on years of experience, is that those who maneuver to be one of the last candidates to be interviewed have a better chance to be remembered, as well as leaving the last great impression, when the vetting process and decision time comes. Very rarely are the first interviewees ever offered the job in a long competition process. I theorize that the reason why is because the interviewers do not remember the candidates as well and must rely on their notes to make a decision. This lack of recall is an additional positive reason for interviewers to add video interviewing and recording to their interviewing protocol, allowing for later review of candidate interviews. The most recent interviewees—those interviewed closest to the interview competition end date—are remembered and are therefore made more offers than their first-interviewed competitors. If you are one of the first, make sure to keep your name as well as your picture in the running by sending updates and follow-ups by e-mail with your LinkedIn button and with a picture, as well as being persistent following up with calls and letters of interest. This is critical if you approached the employer as an applicant by "clicking and sending" rather than being recruited based on your strong ProfessionaliBrand. Ideally, through your great ProfessionaliBrand, you will be a frontrunner right from the get-go—that is, by being considered a candidate rather than an applicant. The bottom line is this: If you heed all the advice in the book you are bound to be a frontrunner regardless of the order in which you are interviewed.

Negotiate Your Best Offer

There are many salary tools online such as Salary.com and professional association tools that will provide you with great information on total compensation for the level, location, and type of position you are considering. Consider all facets in the offer, including vacation, health benefits, potential of stock appreciation, sign-on and performance bonuses, childcare, paid lunch and snacks, fitness center, paid education, and flex time when considering your total package. Determine your minimum acceptable level and negotiate from there. Be a smart negotiator. Determine your "must-haves" and your "nice-to-haves," and negotiate away your nice-to-haves to keep your must-haves. For example, your must-have is three weeks' vacation, versus your nice-to-have $2,000 more in salary and four weeks' vacation. So start your negotiation with the nice-to-have $2,000 more in salary and four weeks' vacation, and be prepared to give it away in order to get the three weeks' vacation—the must-have. The end result is you agree to give away $2,000 and four weeks' vacation if you can get three weeks' vacation, they feel like they won, and you know you won. And—who knows?—you may just get your nice-to-have also.

How to resign and Handle Counter-Offers

There are two important parties involved in a resignation besides yourself: your current employer and your new employer. No one likes to be threatened or, on the other hand, jerked around. Be clear about your intention. If you accept a job make sure to start at the new employer. If you are unsure, do not accept the job, and talk first to your current employer candidly. If it is about getting a raise or a promotion then ask for a raise without mentioning you are shopping around. Do not mention your job offer; no one likes to have a gun held to his head. If you are seeking a counter-offer do not play that game, as it tends to end badly. Speak candidly, and if your employer offers you a raise or promotion, then accept and turn down the new offer. If your employer does not meet your expectations, resign and start your new job. If you accepted the new job, do not accept a counter-offer, and do not bring up anything about your new offer. Simply say, "Thanks. It has been a great opportunity," keep walking, and make the best of your new employer. It is a small world, and the new employer, if shafted, will have a long memory. Also remember things have a tendency to leak out today and spread quickly, and you will be branded as a person who does not keep his agreements. Professional reputation is everything today in the social sphere, so protect it! (You can find more information on how to follow up after an interview and how to resign from a position, including how to write a resignation letter, available at *www.transitiontohired.com/resources.*)

CONCLUSION

YOU ARE CAPABLE BEYOND BELIEF

"THOSE WHO ARE BLESSED WITH THE MOST TALENT DON'T NECESSARILY OUTPER-
FORM EVERYONE ELSE. IT'S THE PEOPLE WITH FOLLOW-THROUGH WHO EXCEL."
—MARY KAY ASH[1]

As I wrap up the writing of this book, another person called me for help today. He is in dire financial straits, he lost his house, and now his automobile is about to be repossessed, unless he can make payments quick. He said he is now ready to start putting himself out there and taking the steps necessary to build his professional image online. Searching the Internet for advertisements just did not pay off.

It breaks my heart to hear stories like these. Having educated him that replying to advertisements was not a job-search strategy but rather a dead end, he still invested 100 percent of his time and energy in a lost cause that cost him and his family dearly. Forget about passion. You are bordering on human tragedy in this case, from a comfortable living making $120,000 a year, to more than one year of unemployment. Why did he remain unemployed for so long? Because he chose not to embrace the new realities of job search.

It is great to read a book, but it is of no use unless you put what you learn into action. Please take the necessary action. Yes, it is scary to try new things and to give up on things that worked in the past, because they are comfortable and familiar, but if they no longer work you must move with the times. The alternative is devastating to your financial well-being as well as your health. Developing an irresistible offer requires tending to your Internet garden. By doing so, your garden will bear fruit in the form of continuous employment and a secure income. A little gardening is a small price to pay to become a sought-after candidate in a Recruiting 3.0 trending world. Yes, it takes effort, but once set up and tweaked, this ProfessionaliBranding process works to get you exposure and build your reputation, and you will never have to look for another job again. Be early to the party and take your ProfessionaliBrand to the next level, and join the ranks of professionals who "get" it before it is too late. Be flexible and consider contracting or consulting. Stay up to date and find the latest tools and best practices by frequenting *www.transitiontohired.com/resources* on a regular basis.

All the calls I get are not bad news stories. I also received two other phone calls today, from professionals exclaiming that they just accepted positions and wanting to thank me for the advice I had passed on. What a feeling!

In the end you may need a job because you need a job, so get your survival job. Once you have one and you can pay the bills, make sure to spend the time to find one you love, because here is another sobering statistic: Research shows conclusively that the most common day for heart attacks is Monday.[2] Statistics spike on Monday mornings in particular: Heart attacks occur between 4 a.m. and 10 a.m. —more than any other six-hour period.[3]

Why do you think that is?

I am neither a social scientist nor a doctor, but I can tell you it's probably as a result of extreme work stress or fear of going to work. Is this a way to live? This is your only time on earth, so choose to *live* life rather than *do* life. Put the effort into finding work that will fulfill your passion. Get the job, venture, or mission that is right for you and that fits you by putting the powerful A-C-T system (alignment, confidence, and tactics) to work for you. It does not matter what you do as long as you love it. As my father frequently says, "To each your own, your ice cream cone, 47 flavors, pick your own."

A quote by author Marianne Williamson sums up the book best:

Our Deepest Fear

> Our deepest fear is not that we are inadequate. Our deepest fear is that we are powerful beyond measure. It is our light, not our darkness that most frightens us. We ask ourselves, who am I to be brilliant, gorgeous, talented, fabulous? Actually, who are you not to be? You are a child of God. Your playing small does not serve the world. There is nothing enlightened about shrinking so that other people won't feel insecure around you. We are all meant to shine, as children do. We were born to make manifest the glory of God that is within us. It's not just in some of us; it's in everyone. And as we let our own light shine, we unconsciously give other people permission to do the same. As we are liberated from our own fear, our presence automatically liberates others.[4]

You are capable beyond belief!

It is now up to you to shine bright, announce your greatness to the world, and fulfill your passion every day!

NOTES

Introduction

1. Dictionary of Quotes Website, *www.dictionary-quotes.com/your-work-is-to-discover-your-work-and-then-with-all-your-heart-to-give-yourself-to-it-buddha/.* Retrieved August 9, 2011.

2. Morello, C. "Results of Polls on Job Satisfaction Are at Odds." *Washington Post* Website, *www.washingtonpost.com/wp-dyn/content/article/2010/01/05/AR2010010503977.html.* Retrieved July 23, 2011.

3. Belkic, K.L., P.A. Landsbergis, et al. "Is Job Strain a Major Source of Cardiovascular Disease Risk?" *Scandinavian Journal of Work, Environment and Health*, 30 (2), 2004: 85–128.

4. Marchione, M. "Women with Stressful Jobs Have 40 Percent Higher Heart Risks. Fear of Losing a Job Also Raises Heart Risk, Shows Largest Study of its Kind." MSNBC Website, *www.msnbc.msn.com/id/40182278/ns/health-womens_health/t/women-stressful-jobs-have-percent-higher-heart-risks/*. Retrieved November 18, 2010.

5. Commodity jobs are jobs that do not require very specialized skills, for example: cashier, fast-food clerk, nad telemarketer.

Chapter 1

1. Buddha. BrainyQuote.com, *www.brainyquote.com/quotes/quotes/b/buddha118245.html*. Retrieved October 25, 2011.

2. Greene, Brenda, and Coleen Byrne. *Web 2.0 Job Finder* (Pompton Plains, N.J.: Career Press, 2010), p. 47.

3. Pierson, D. Brain Sync Website, *www.brainsync.com/news/scientific-endorsements.html*. Retrieved September 24, 2011.

4. Hutchison, M. *Megabrain: New Tools and Techniques for Brain Growth and Mind Expansion*. Brain Sync Website, *www.brainsync.com/news/scientific-endorsements.html*. Retrieved September 24, 2011.

5. Taub, MD, Edward A., spokesperson for the American Medical Association's National Stop Smoking Campaign. Brain Sync Website, *www.brainsync.com/news/scientific-endorsements.html*. Retrieved September 24, 2011.

Chapter 2

1. Socrates. Philosophy Paradise Website, *www.philosophyparadise.com/quotes/socrates.html*. Retrieved August 10, 2011.

2. Table 2.1 was adapted from ADV Advanced Technical Services Inc. Candidate Profiler.

3. Table 2.2 was created from concept from TTI Performance Systems Ltd.

Chapter 3

1. Anatole France. BrainyQuote.com, *www.brainyquote.com/quotes/quotes/a/anatolefra161340.html*. Retrieved August 10, 2011.

Chapter 4

1. Arnold Schwarzenegger, as quoted in *Mind Power Into the 21st Century* by John Kehoe (Vancouver, Canada: Zoetic Inc., 1997), p. 13.

2. Ranganathan, V.K, V. Siemionow, J.Z. Liu, V. Sahgal, and G.H. Yue. "From Mental Power to Muscle Power—Gaining Strength by Using the Mind." *Neuropsychologia* 42.7 (2004): 944–56. U.S. National Library of Medicine, National Institutes of Health Website, *www.ncbi.nlm.nih.gov/pubmed/14998709*. Retrieved July 28, 2011.

3. Reiser, M., D. Büsch, and J. Munzert. "Strength Gains by Motor Imagery with Different Ratios of Physical to Mental Practice." *Frontiers in Psychology* 2 (2001): 194. Epub.

4. Montapert, Alfred A. BrainyQuote.com, *www.brainyquote.com/quotes/quotes/a/alfredamo166039.html*. Retrieved October 25, 2011.

5. Gauntlett, D. University of Westminster, Art Lab Website, *www.artlab.org.uk/visualisation.htm*. Retrieved July 29, 2011.

6. Einstein, Albert. BrainyQuote.com, *www.brainyquote.com/quotes/quotes/a/alberteins129815.html*. Retrieved August 10, 2011.

7. Venuto, T. "The New Visualization Breakthrough: Mental Training Tactics for Health, and Fitness Success." Health and Alternative Healing Methods Website, *www.gems4friends.com/fitness/the-new-visualization-breakthroug.html*. Retrieved July 30, 2011.

8. Greenhouse, C. "O. Carl Simonton: Alternative Healing." *Ode Magazine* Website, 2007, *www.odemagazine.com/doc/60/alternative-healing/*. Retrieved August 9, 2011.

9. Andreasen, N.C. *The Creative Brain: The Science of Genius* (New York: Plume, 2006), p. 103.

10. Ness, E. "The Reticular Activating System—Your Brain's Unique Screening Device." The Write Event Website, 2007, *graciousliving.typepad.com/the_write_event/2007/08/the-reticular-a.html.* Retrieved July 30, 2011.

Chapter 5

1. Buddha. BrainyQuote.com, *www.brainyquote.com/quotes/quotes/b/buddha120914.html.* Retrieved August 10, 2011.

2. "Job & Career Networking" Careerplaybook.com, *www.career-playbook.com/guide/networking.asp.* Retrieved July 31, 2011.

3. Schawbel, D. (2011). "5 Reasons Why Your Online Presence Will Replace Your Resume in 10 Years." Forbes.com. *www.forbes.com/sites/danschawbel/2011/02/21/5-reasons-why-your-online-presence-will-replace-your-resume-in-10-years/.* Retrieved October 20, 2011.

4. Adams, S. "The Myth of Job Listings." Forbes.com, *www.forbes.com/sites/susanadams/2011/02/15/the-myth-of-job-listings/.* Retrieved on October 20, 2011.

5. "Job-Board Journalism: Selling out the American Job Hunter." Google Answers Website. *www.answers.google.com/answers/threadview/id/580853.html.* Retrieved July 20, 2011.

6. Schonfeld, E. "Indeed Slips Past Monster, Now Largest Job Site By Unique Visitors." Techcrunch.com. *www.techcrunch.com/2010/11/17/indeed-monster-largest-job-site/.* Retrieved November 17, 2011.

7. Hill, K. "What Prospective Employers Hope to See in Your Facebook Account: Creativity, Well-Roundedness, & 'Chastity.'" Forbes.com, 2011. *www.forbes.com/sites/kashmirhill/2011/10/03/what-prospective-employers-hope-to-see-in-your-facebook-account-creativity-well-roundedness-chastity/.* Retrieved October 4, 2011.

8. Ibid.

9. Ibid.

10. King, S., A. Townsend, and C. Ockels. "The Intuit Future of Small Business Series, SR-1037A." *http-download.intuit.com/http.intuit/CMO/intuit/futureofsmallbusiness/SR-1037_intuit_SmallBiz_Demog.pdf.* 2007. Retrieved August 8, 2011.

11. Schoen, J. "Boomers Face Stark Choices in Bleak Economy, Prolonged Economic Collapse Leaves Little Time to Reinvent, Recover, Rebuild." MSNBC Webiste, *sys12-today.msnbc.msn.com/id/29535417/ns/business-us_business/*. Retrieved October 4, 2011.

Chapter 6

1. Cooley, Mason. BrainyQuote.com, *www.brainyquote.com/quotes/quotes/m/masoncoole394820.html*. Retrieved August 10, 2011.

2. Nordhaug, O., and K. Gronhaug. *The International Journal of Human Resource Management*, 5 (1994): 89–106.

3. Kessler, Robin, and Linda A. Strasburg. *Competency-Based Resumes* (Franklin Lakes, N.J.: Career Press, 2005).

4. Schroeter, K. "Competence Literature Review, Competency & Credentialing Institute." Scribd.com, 2008. *www.scribd.com/doc/24691311/Competence-Lit-Review-1*. Retrieved July 21, 2011.

5. "The Reppler Effect: Managing Your Online Image Across Social Networks." *blog.reppler.com/2011/09/27/managing-your-online-image-across-social-netowrks*. Retrieved December 17, 2011.

6. Adapted, enlarged list inspired by Boston College, Resume Action Words. *www.bc.edu/offices/careers/skills/resumes/verbs.html*. Retrieved July 20, 2011.

7. "Controls Hardware Design Engineer." TotalJobs.com, *www.totaljobs.com/JobSeeking/Controls-Hardware-Design-Engineer_job50943439*. Retrieved August 1, 2011.

8. Kessler and Strasburg. *Competency-Based Resumes*.

Chapter 7

1. Brit Hume. BrainyQuote.com, *www.brainyquote.com/quotes/quotes/b/brithume271130.html*. Retrieved October 25, 2011.

2. "Web 2.0." Webopedia, *www.webopedia.com/TERM/W/Web_2_point_0.html*. Retrieved June 26, 2011.

3. Aronson, E., T.D. Wilson, and A.M. Akert. *Social Psychology 5th ed.* (Upper Saddle River, N.J.: Prentice Hall, 2005).

4. Hill, K. "What Prospective Employers Hope To See In Your Facebook Account: Creativity, Well-Roundedness, & 'Chastity.'" Forbes.com, 2011. *www.forbes.com/sites/kashmirhill/2011/10/03/ what-prospective-employers-hope-to-see-in-your-facebook-account-creativity-well-roundedness-chastity/*. Retrieved October 4, 2011.

5. Ibid.

6. Microsoft Privacy Team. "Microsoft Releases a Study on Data Privacy Day." Microsoft TechNet Website, 2010. *blogs.technet. com/b/privacyimperative/archive/2010/01/27/microsoft-releases-a-study-on-data-privacy-day.aspx*. Retrieved June 26, 2011.

7. Hill, K. "Feds Okay Start-up That Monitors Employees' Internet and Social Media Footprints." Forbes.com, 2011. *www.forbes.com/ sites/kashmirhill/2011/06/15/start-up-that-monitors-employees-internet-and-social-media-footprints-gets-gov-approval/2/*. Retrieved June 15, 2011.

8. MeshHire.com. *www.MeshHire.com*. Retrieved August 10, 2011.

9. Needleman, S. E. "Recruiting 3.0: Web Advances Change the Landscape." *Wall Street Journal* Website, 2008. *online.wsj.com/article/SB120173287043830005.html*. Retrieved July 30, 2011.

10. Gandhi, S. "IBM Dives into Second Life, Meeting, Collaborating, and Brainstorming in a Virtual World." IBM Website, 2010. *www. ibm.com/developerworks/opensource/library/os-social-secondlife/?ca=drs-*. Retrieved August 8, 2011.

11. Athavaley, A. "A Job Interview You Don't Have to Show Up For. Microsoft, Verizon, Others Use Virtual Worlds to Recruit; Dressing Avatars for Success." *Wall Street Journal* (Personal Journal) Website, 2007. *online.wsj.com/article/SB118229876637841321. html*. Retrieved October 23, 2011.

12. Greene, Brenda, and Coleen Byrne. *Web 2.0 Job Finder* (Pompton Plains, N.J.: Career Press, 2010), p. 47.

13. Kidd, K. "Now on the Auction Block: Work." Thestar.com, 2011. *www.thestar.com/news/insight/article/1070444--now-on-the-auction-block-work*. Retrieved October 15, 2011.

14. Goodwin, D. "Search Engine Watch, Top Google Result Gets 36.4% of Clicks" [Study]. Search Engine Watch Website, 2011. *searchenginewatch.com/article/2049695/Top-Google-Result-Gets-36.4-of-Clicks-Study*. Retrieved July 2, 2011.

15. Gawronski, B., R.J. Rydell, B. Vervliet, and J. DeHouwer. "Generalization Versus Contextualization in Automatic Evaluation." *Journal of Experimental Psychology: General,* Advance online publication. 2010. doi: 10.1037/a0020315.

16. Zarrella, D. *Zarrella's Hierarchy of Contagiousness: The Science, Design, and Engineering of Contagious Ideas.* The Domino Project, 2011.

17. Ibid.

18. Postrel, V. "A Small Circle of Friends." Forbes.com, 2007. *members. forbes.com/free_forbes/2007/0507/204.html?boxes=custom.*Retrieved July 31, 2011.

19. Arrington, M. "Tech Crunch Facebook Video Chat v. Google Hangouts: It's No Contest." TechCrunch.com, 2011. *techcrunch. com/2011/07/06/facebook-video-chat-google-hangouts/.* Retrieved August 8, 2011.

Chapter 8

1. Keller, Helen. BrainyQuote.com, *www.brainyquote.com/quotes/ quotes/h/helenkelle382259.html.* Retrieved August 10, 2011.

Chapter 9

1. Kennedy, John F. BrainyQuote.com, *www.brainyquote.com/quotes/ quotes/j/johnfkenn109216.html.* Retrieved August 10, 2011.

2. Pankow, G. "Voicemail Surfing: A Comprehensive Guide on Using Voicemail to Circumvent Gatekeepers." RW Stearns, Inc. Website, 2009. *www.rwstearns.com/tpl/Voicemail_Surfing_White_ Paper_01-15-09.pdf.* Retrieved January 20, 2011.

3. "U.S. Census Bureau, Statistics About Business Size (Including Small Business)." *www.census.gov.econ/smallbus.html.* Retrieved December 26, 2011.

Chapter 10

1. Murphy, Arthur. *The Works of Samuel Johnson, Volume 6.* Biblio-Bazaar (January 30, 2007), p. 154.

Chapter 11

1. Rohn, Jim. BrainyQuote.com, *www.brainyquote.com/quotes/quotes/j/jimrohn132151.html.* Retrieved August 10, 2011.

Conclusion

1. Ash, Mary Kay. BrainyQuote.com, *www.brainyquote.com/quotes/quotes/m/marykayash138619.html.* Retrieved August 10, 2011.

2. "Monday morning bad for your health." CNN.com, 2005. *edition.cnn.com/2005/BUSINESS/02/03/monday.pressure/index.html.* Retrieved August 10, 2011.

3. Doctors, The, with Mariskavan Aalst. *The Doctors 5-Minute Health Fixes: The Prescription for a Lifetime of Great Health* (Emmaus, Pa.: Rodale, 2011), p. 24.

4. Williamson, M. *A Return To Love: Reflections on the Principles of Course in Miracles* (New York: HarperCollins, 1992), pp. 190–191.

INDEX

ABOUT THE AUTHOR

Paul Hill is recognized as a new breed of job-search expert, educating professionals and corporations on the implementation of Recruiting 3.0 strategies. He is dedicated to educating, coaching, and guiding professionals to be proactive in job search by adopting ProfessionaliBranding best practices through his work as principal of TransitionToHired.

He has built an award-winning record as a leader in the international placement industry for more than 25 years. His company, ADV Advanced Technical Services Inc., won numerous National Personnel Associates awards for outstanding production. He is positively impacting the lives of professionals as well as new immigrants to Canada and the United States through his work at TransitiontoHired and the launch of "Be Irresistible," a step-by-step guide to proactive job search.

Also from CAREER PRESS

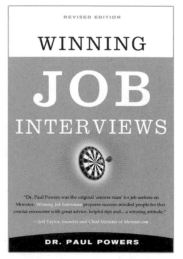

WINNING JOB INTERVIEWS
Revised Edition
Paul Powers
EAN 978-1601630889

WORK AT HOME NOW
Christine Durst & Michael Haaren
EAN 978-1601630919

HIGHTLY EFFECTIVE NETWORKING
Orville Pierson
EAN 978-1601630506

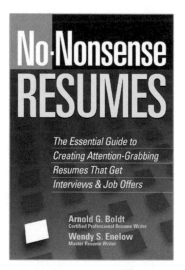

NO-NONSENSE RESUMES
Wendy Enelow & Arnold Boldt
EAN 978-1564149053

TO ORDER CALL 1-800-227-3371 OR VISIT CAREERPRESS.COM

Also from CAREER PRESS

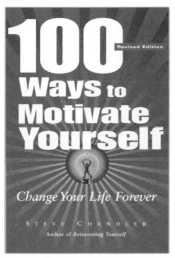

100 Ways to Motivate Yourself
Revised Edition
Steve Chandler
EAN 978-1564147752

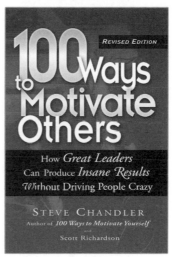

100 Ways to Motivate Others
Revised Edition
Steve Chandler
EAN 978-1564149923

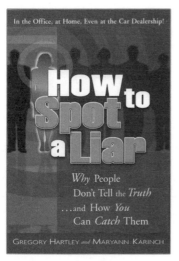

How to Spot a Liar
Gregory Hartley &
Maryann Karinch
EAN 978-1564148407

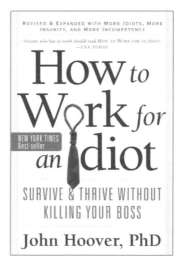

How to Work for an Idiot
John Hoover
EAN 978-1601631916

To Order Call 1-800-227-3371 or visit CareerPress.com

EAGLE VALLEY LIBRARY DISTRICT
P.O. BOX 240   600 BROADWAY
EAGLE, CO 81631   (970) 328-8800